FOR
MAGAZINES

WRITING FOR MAGAZINES

Jill Dick

Second Edition

A & C Black · London

Second edition published 1996
First edition published 1994
A & C Black (Publishers) Limited
35 Bedford Row, London WC1R 4JH

ISBN 0-7136-4485-0

A CIP catalogue record for this book
is available from the British Library

Cover illustration by Conny Jude

Typeset in 10½ on 12pt Palatino
Printed in Great Britain by Redwood Books,
Trowbridge, Wilts.

To Jim

Contents

• Will a magazine steal my ideas? • How can I improve
my vocabulary? • Which word-processor do you
recommend? • How do I know when to use capital
letters? • What do magazines pay and where do I find
a list of the standard rates?

Introduction

This second edition of *Writing for Magazines* has been thoroughly up-dated and covers everything you need to know in practical terms. Letters from readers of the earlier edition tell me it was a revelation to them, with pages of insider knowledge that makes the difference between triumph and failure – and with this edition we go further.

Here you will find all the help and information you need if you want to write non-fiction for magazines. Many thousands of different magazines publish articles on every conceivable subject, written to appeal to readers with all sorts of interests, from all backgrounds, of all ages and every level of education – or none; the intellectual and the man-in-the-street, you, me and the next person you meet. Everyone is a 'reader' to the magazine world and every 'reader' is the person you will be writing for.

Are you interested in people and what happens to them? Do you want to know what goes on around you and in the wider world – and to talk about it to other people? Are you fascinated by other folk's hobbies and experiences? No wonder we writers are always busy; there is so much to write about in so many different ways. International events, domestic issues and every concept of life are brought right into our homes; it is easy to be aware of everything happening around us. We have total freedom to write what we like – and this sort of writing is simply a craft that can be learned, with perseverance and discipline. The people who write for magazines were all untrained beginners at one time. They learned how magazines are put together, what editors want and how to provide it. Freelances who don't regularly go into magazine offices sell their work from their own homes (or sometimes from offices established so several like-minded writers can share the same equipment, with minimal expense for each) and run their affairs as a part-time hobby or small business.

As well as the huge article field, there are many other outlets for non-fiction writers: interviewing, compiling competitions, covering arts events for local and regional magazines, running a regular children's page, a cookery or a gardening column, supplying sports features or merely writing fillers or letters to the editor.

There is plenty to write about and no shortage of places to sell what you write. Besides the large number of magazines published in the UK each year a great many more published in America and other English-speaking countries are also wide open to freelance writers. Nor must we now confine ourselves to English-speaking markets: computer programs that translate copy as it is read have transformed the changing of text into almost any other language – and perhaps the big question of syndication is still awaiting your discovery.

Any written item or piece of work is referred to as a 'story' in the magazine world so in this book don't suddenly worry that we're talking about fiction. Likewise the word 'copy' simply means any matter eventually to be set in type ready for printing; anything written, whether typed, word-processed or even hand-written (for letters to the editor, for example) is 'copy'.

If you are reading this book you must already have a strong writing urge in your heart, and that is the very first essential for success. And you won't be discouraged when I remind you that to achieve publication, especially regularly, demands more than a heart-felt desire, however burning: a great deal more. There are many other people competing against you – including some who have worked on the staff of magazines – and there will be days when all your hard work will seem fruitless. You may wonder whether it is worth going on – but also in your heart you will know the answer is a definite 'yes'. If you've yet to achieve publication the most wonderful euphoria in the world lies just ahead of you. For any published writer will tell you there's nothing quite like the exhilaration of seeing your own work in print and knowing that for that day or week or month, at least, many thousands of readers will be reading what you have written. Freelance writing for magazines is exciting, absorbing, and – I can't deny it – sometimes frustrating. But when you're an old hand at the craft, with countless published articles to your credit, the pleasure of such a moment never diminishes.

There have been many changes in the magazine world in the past few years. Small and sometimes barely perceptible alterations used to be introduced gradually; until you compared one issue with another published six or twelve months earlier you might not have been aware that there had been any changes. But dramatic developments in the world of communications have revolutionised magazines: the technological revolution is here. Children take to it at primary school level, to every office worker with the need to communicate it is as easy as picking up a pencil and to writers – to us it is a blessing. But it means far more than writing at our word-processors; it give us easy contact with magazine editors and staff, it offers us the chance to research a world-wide base of source material we never even knew existed let alone found accessible and it lets us keep our copy safely at home and send it anywhere in the world (sometimes without even committing it to paper) at the touch of a button. All the same I can't pretend the advance of technology has brought no problems to writers. Complex concerns – some covering our rights and responsibilities in the electronic world – are fully discussed in this book, together with every aspect touching the lives of working freelances in these high-tech days. To gain every scrap of help and information you'll also find the answers to Frequently Asked Questions on page 183 and on every page you'll find tips and hints, no matter where you are on the ladder of success. What's more important, you'll enjoy getting there.

Jill Dick

1
Surveying the field

Imagine looking at a sheet of paper the size of a tennis court and knowing you have to fill it with words and pictures every week. This is the approximate area editors of weekly magazines face regularly and it's a wonder any can sleep in their beds at night for worrying about how they're going to do it and what they're going to fill it with. For not only must the space be filled, it must be attractively filled, nay, *irresistibly* filled, if existing readers are to be kept happy and new ones attracted.

Fortunately for the sanity of editors (and those of monthly magazines have a less frenetic task though they do face other pressures not bearing on their weekly cousins) a pattern of work is well-established whereby there is never a wholly unfilled block of white space to be faced. The system depends on a methodically calculated 'lead time' which for most weekly magazines means starting on a particular issue at least three months before its publication date.

By early February *People's Friend* (officially titled *The People's Friend*) has a full 'programme book' planned up to the end of the year and beyond, at least as far as the serial programme and special features (general interest, craft, cookery, knitting etc) are concerned. The editor works two months head in putting the weekly magazine together. That means on February 23, say, once the final list of advertisements is to hand, fiction is chosen for the April 20 edition. It's essential that topical stories and features, like those relevant to Christmas and Easter, are submitted several months in advance. We non-fiction writers have to move quickly!

Having a very detailed and clearly defined plan of what they hope to publish is another aid to peace of mind in editorial offices – even though they don't always receive it.

Bella guidelines

Here, for example, is a guide to what the editor of *Bella* currently wants with pointers freelance contributors should attend to before submitting copy; think of it as your introduction to this popular weekly for women. Whatever you write for *Bella* never use material taken from old cuttings without tracing the source and updating the information. Using previously published material without bothering to check the story behind it is inviting rejection and trying to sell work containing 'dead' copy is wasting everyone's time.

Newsy, authoritative and carefully-researched features of 1500 words are welcomed: trends, social issues and syndromes – light, heavy or off-beat. Illustrate different aspects of your chosen theme with three strong and detailed case histories. But cross-check them with your editor or commissioning editor before writing your copy: it may be (for a number of reasons beyond your control) that the stories you wish to use will not be acceptable. Support your work with comments, facts and figures from named experts – and make use of information boxes with helpline telephone numbers where appropriate. Provide adequate backup for a proper insight into the causes of people's problems, how they feel and how they may be helped.

For copy about people and interviews all quoted facts must be correct: check the accuracy and spelling of Christian and surnames, addresses, ages (give dates of birth rather than ages at the time of writing: the latter changes, the former doesn't), marital status, the number and names of children, dates of important events and precise legal details of court cases. In addition, always give the names, addresses and telephone numbers of interviewees at the end of your copy – and add a word count.

Bella wants non-fiction stories in several categories:

Real life (1,000 words) may be triumph-over-tragedy, off-beat or adventure, involving animals, families or individuals – and usually about extraordinary things happening to ordinary people. Ask interviewees how they felt at the time of the event central to your story, establish it in sound chronological order, and use first person quotes in reporting facts and feelings. Small details, personality traits and natural fresh emotion are very important.

Families (1,000 words) involving any family unit – parents, babies, siblings, grandparents etc. The emphasis should be on shared experiences and how family members support and interact with each other in times of drama, adventure or overcoming tragedy. Use emotive quotes – something heart-tugging – from all the family, especially from children if appropriate, and make male members speak up as well.

My own story (1,400 words): first person intimate stories packed with emotion and small but telling detail. You need to question interviewees with sensitivity, revealing how they felt and reacted at every stage of the story and incorporating telling touches to reveal how their experiences were unique.

Scales of justice (1,000 words) features fights for justice or compensation in or out of court, with full explanations of the emotional turmoil at the heart of each case. But keep the reader guessing as to the outcome! Provide exact details of legal charges and sentences. It almost goes without saying that all information must be true and accurate and that dates, and the names of courts, judges and anyone else involved must be correct. Tell how the cases affected your subjects' lives and what the long-term effects have been on them and their families.

The secret I must share (1,000 words): intimate confessions in the first person, light-hearted or serious, often carrying a real burden of emotional guilt.

Talking point (800-900 words) needs well-reasoned debates examining differing aspects of live case histories. Use only original relevant quotes and keep your argument concise, with at least two case histories and two experts, supported by up-to-date facts and statistics.

Blushes are third person funny, sexy or saucy stories about embarrassing incidents, written in a bright and bouncy style with dialogue to show reactions and behaviour. Names and ages may be changed.

Did you expect such precise and vivid requirements from one of our leading weekly periodicals? It's just the first taste of market study.

A lot of white space . . .

With some 12-13,000 separate magazines published in the UK alone every year, mostly appearing weekly or monthly (and many more published at less frequent intervals), there must be at least 400,000 editions to fill, plus all the overseas and international titles.

A recent magazine survey shows writing to be the most popular home-based occupation. If you want to help fill some of those magazines you need only learn what thousands of other magazines writers have already learned. The contributor an editor longs to hear from identifies with readers, understands what they want, doesn't patronise or belittle them, feeds them with new ideas and leaves them feeling happier with themselves and their way of life than they were before they bought the magazine. Such a contributor, I need hardly add, is never out of work and enjoys endless interest in life.

How it all began

Magazine-readership increased enormously in the nineteenth century, mainly due to the development of the railways. The first W H Smith bookstall was opened at Euston station in 1848 and twenty-two years later came the Education Act which vastly extended the prospects of reading (and writing) among the majority of the population who had previously been denied such opportunities. Magazine publishing started to grow and stalls selling magazines and periodicals became familiar sights on railway stations in England and Wales.

Trains attracted crowds of people and by the first years of the twentieth century W H Smith had set up more than 140 bookstalls at stations or on the paths leading to them. In Scotland Edinburgh bookseller John Menzies opened the first of a rapidly-expanding string of bookstalls, eventually also taking over Wymans, and railway travellers were delighted countrywide. Further benefits lay ahead for the magazine business.

Before this time published titles had been subject to a hefty tax on all advertisements carried in their pages – which made many expensive and therefore limited in their appeal. A high proportion of the general public who could read and desperately wanted to read magazines could not afford to do so. In the mid-nineteenth century Palmerston's government had bowed to the complaints about the so-called 'Taxes on knowledge' and abolished the stamp

duty on newspapers and magazines. Now the way was open and
the elements were in place for a surge in magazine prosperity:
better transport, particularly by rail, enabled the faster distribution of raw materials and printed matter, while an eager reading
public was waiting to buy the results in quantity. Periodical
publishing meant business as never before.

But competition was fierce (always a healthy sign for writers
and readers, although some of the former may not agree).
Companies heading the scene during the first half of this century
– George Newnes, Alfred Harmsworth, C. Arthur Pearson, Amal-
gamated Press, Odhams, Hulton, Fleetway and D. C. Thomson of
Dundee among them – found heady improvements in printing
techniques added strength to their empires as well as income to
their pockets. To sort out circulation and readership figures
claimed by rival publishers the Audit Bureau of Circulation
began its work. It continues to this day from Black Prince Yard,
207-209 High Street, Berkhamsted, Herts HP4 1AD.

The need to monitor readership was also important; advertisers had to be sure they were reaching their targets and that the
money spent in buying advertising space in magazine pages was
not wasted. Whether they knew or cared about it, readers had to
be put into fairly rigorous classes to assess their buying propen-
sities. Reader-classification was born.

Advertising is king

Now, as in earlier years, the value of studying magazine advertisements cannot be over-emphasised. Whether studying as a
potential contributor or merely browsing as a casual reader,
never underestimate their power. Revenue from advertising
accounts for more than half the income of consumer magazines.
Advertisers rent pages and use the space to sell their products to
readers. Of course those products will be in keeping with the
topics covered in the magazines and the obvious predilections of
their buyers.

So how is the freelance to interpret what advertisements tell
us? Advertising agencies know exactly where readers fit into
today's society. Their success depends on making accurate judgments about who the readers of any given title will be – and
writers can learn a good deal from these judgments. The advertisements reflect precisely defined socioeconomic categories –
that 'reader classification' mentioned above. While not all readers
fall into the same group in every respect so even the best adver-

tising agencies do not please everyone all the time – but it is foolish to ignore the benefits their expert studies can offer us.

These socioeconomic groups are clearly defined and everyone falls into the appropriate category by a practical evaluation of many aspects of our lives, some of which may change over the years and cause us to 'move' from one group to another. Among the factors deciding our place in the classification are age, occupation, education (our own and our children's), background, the type of house we live in, the cars we drive and the holidays we choose. It all adds up to an analysis of our income, capital and, most importantly, our spending power. Did you realise such a cold-blooded assessment of us and our habits was at work? Rest assured there is nothing sinister in it and everything advertising agencies discover about us is already well-documented elsewhere (some of it in the records of the Inland Revenue, alas).

Resilience

Many magazines were among the casualties as paper was rationed and staffing levels reduced when Britain was at war in 1939. Getting anything to read was difficult and magazines, particularly women's magazines, were passed from hand to hand until they literally fell apart. By the time the war ended only 25–30 leading weekly and monthly titles were regularly published and owners and publishers realised the market had changed a great deal. But there was a challenging and vigorous optimism in the air and it would not wait; behind it was a new sort of reader – and that classification embraced virtually everybody. In the magazine world new enterprise and initiative were on their way and keeping pace with them was the only route to success. Countless titles were born to short lives after expensive launches.

Then another threat dealt the hard-working magazine business a major blow: commercial television came to snatch mouthfuls of advertising revenue from their hands. The publishers responded by banding together; unity was strength and made the best use of printing costs, distribution channels, advertising and sales techniques. Magazines appeared for sale in places where they had not been seen before: in supermarkets where their tempting glossy covers would attract the eyes of housewives waiting at the checkouts, at airports and even on buses in a few lowly populated areas. International publications, mainly from the United States, sold well. There was a surging teenage market (as a result of the 'baby boom' after the war) and everywhere publishers, owners, advertisers, distributors, editors and all their staff worked as never before to capture readers and survive. It was a question of work hard or fold – and many folded.

Today's scene

When talking about who leads the field in periodical publishing in the UK, ranking is achieved by an assessment of retail revenue – and that involves ABC-verified sales multiplied by cover prices. In other words, the amount of money spent on any particular magazine is the determining factor.

The top ten magazine publishing groups, as I write, are:

1 IPC
2 EMAP
3 BBC Magazines
4 Bauer
5 Future Publishing
6 The National Magazine Company
7 Reader's Digest
8 Haymarket Press
9 D.C. Thomson
10 The Economist

Do you notice number 4 – Bauer? In the 1980s yet another new development gave established publishers here a jolt. European companies moved in. The German company Gruner & Jahr had bought the overseas rights to the American magazine *Parents* and were franchising it to several countries in Europe, including Britain. Later they launched *Prima* and then *Best*. Bauer, another German publisher and the largest in the country, immediately launched *Bella* (whose current requirements are detailed on page 5). Other titles appeared in English from companies based in France, Spain, Holland, Italy, Australia ... magazine publishing in this country would never be the same. You can read more about the current international scene for writers in Chapter 7.

Even at the worst of the recession more magazines were being launched than closed and media experts predict yet stronger growth in magazine publishing in the years ahead. However many titles there are published now and wherever they may be found, between them they cover all the interests of every potential reader.

Your heart and your head

Are you made of the right stuff? Have you the necessary self-discipline to work by yourself, even or especially at times when you would rather not be working at all? Do you have an appreciation of and a feel for words and an inner sense about the rhythm of language? Is your mind open and not closed to anything? Are you practical? For regular sales and income, you'll be wise to set yourself targets in a carefully-laid plan Think of how much time you can allow for researching a topic, in negotiations and sales-talk with editors, in market research and in the actual writing. I believe many good journalists, without arrogance or any hint of 'preciousness', instinctively see everything while standing just a little apart from it. It's as if they were watching with detachment (and that's very different from disinterest) even when they are themselves caught up in exciting or dramatic affairs.

What kind of journalist are you going to be? A 'news-fattener' or a specialist? News stories on their own are not the stuff of magazines because the timing of magazine production is not geared to reporting news: an angler is electrocuted when his hook catches a power cable – the bald facts of when, where and to whom this tragedy occurred make headlines and paragraphs in newspapers. But to fatten the story with features about the dangers of angling or whether participants in Britain's most popular sport ought to be licensed and insured before casting their lines – these and innumerable associated topics could make acceptable copy for suitably-chosen magazines.

Perhaps you prefer to specialise, sticking to articles on a single theme? Will you write exclusively about cookery, a particular sport, renovating old houses or the red deer of Scotland? I must warn you that specialisation can rob you of the advantages of learning from wider experience and make the selling of copy a greater uphill struggle than it otherwise might be. The way to avoid the danger of exclusivity (at least until you become a nationally or internationally known specialist on your chosen topic) is to be ready to cover a wide variety of topics, while placing special emphasis on a handful of themes. Success is most likely to come to those who enjoy their work, especially early in their careers. Later, with mounting experience, you will being to learn what is probably a more professional attitude to writing: to enjoy it in a different sense. To equate 'success' with the fees received for a piece of work, its prominence and importance in its published venue – and the pleasure you have had in writing it – to 'enjoy' your work in that sense marks your real progress as a published writer. By then you will have learned that whatever you choose to write simply because it will earn you a good cheque will also be setting you a welcome challenge.

In this book there is help in finding ideas (more usable ones than you can develop in a lifetime) and wads of marketing information on how to sell your work and do the research necessary to give it substance and strength. A new section on electronic help in research explores the use of on-line services (with easy-to-follow explanations for writers new to the modem) and there is a comprehensive chapter on essential ingredients of style and structure. The skill of interviewing is explored in depth, how to present and dispatch work to editors are clearly explained and a variety of other writing outlets are also discussed. Another chapter on marketing extends to selling work overseas and how to supply pictures to illustrate your articles is fully investigated.

The business side of writing is crucial to success. You need to know how editors think, whether or not to send query letters, how to get commissioned work and what rights you hold in what you have written; discussing fees, keeping records, claiming expenses, tax liability, syndication, training for the job – these and many other important business matters are discussed in these pages.

If you feel rather lost at first, without experience of writing for magazines and wondering how you are going to gain success in what is without doubt a highly competitive world, take heart: in 1984 *The Economist* invited four multi-national chairmen, four dustmen, four Oxford undergraduates and four finance members from the Organisation for Economic Co-operation and Development to give their views on several topics of the day. All four groups were invited to make predictions that would apply ten years hence on three scores: the value of the pound against the US dollar, the price of a barrel of oil, and an assessment of the gross domestic product of Singapore compared with that of Australia. The dustmen won the first two rounds and tied in first place with the company chairmen in forecasting that the gross national product of Singapore would overtake that of Australia – as it has. The others vowed such a thing was impossible.

No matter how many books you read or how much guidance you absorb, success in writing for magazines depends on three simple factors:

1 Dogged perseverance. (But without (2) you will be flogging a dead horse.)

2 Quality writing. (But without (3) even this will be born to blush unseen.)

3 Dedicated market study and learning how to take the bull by the horns in a professional approach. (And that includes not bespattering your copy with effortless clichés.)

2
Ideas

Get an idea and find a market. Or find the market and then think up an idea? Which way is easier and eventually produces more sales? I have found the answer depends on two main components: your level of experience in writing and selling, and how well you and your intended market know each other. There are other considerations, of course, which lead some writers to vow getting the idea leads to the market – while others insist the reverse is true. I spoke to magazine writers of varied expertise and achievement who agreed to share their views with me. I asked them what they felt should come first – an idea, a market, or anything else – and why. This is what I found:

Most of the beginners or near-beginners put their priorities firmly on ideas and then thought of where to sell while a few claimed they never had any worthwhile ideas without looking at magazines first.

A success rate of 40% (i.e. acceptance of at least 40% of stories submitted) I defined as 'getting-established', and the majority of those in this category stated finding the markets should come before any writing was done at all. A couple liked to keep the two balls of markets and ideas juggling in the air at the same time, not insisting either was more important than the other.

The last group I questioned were more practised than the others, being former magazine staffers although their staff jobs did not involve writing. Half admitted to earning 'enough to live on' (their quotes), some were happy with 'satisfactory part-time earnings' and the others didn't reveal their success in money terms. All stressed how hard they worked for their rewards – 'harder than beginners ever appreciate' they said – and two considered the rewards were so poor they were thinking of giving up if the situation didn't improve. Regarding the chicken/egg position they were unanimous: *of course* finding the market comes first. So much for the voice of experience: it is one we would all do well to heed.

As for my second point about how well you and your intended market know each other – that can be of prime importance. Once you have made a few sales to a particular magazine the editor will get to know the type of copy (written work) you can supply, the speed at which you can or will work and – most importantly of all, perhaps – your reliability. No longer will you be starting from scratch with an unknown editor of an unfamiliar market: the scales will be weighed in your favour. But beware! Complacency loses sales and although you can feel more comfortable in your relationship with the editor when you have already contributed to the magazine, try sending work that is below the standard required and you'll be rejected as quickly as any raw beginner submitting unsuitable copy.

Ideas are all

Writers without ideas are stuck in sterility: you can't get your mind working, let alone your typing fingers. A few writers claim the mere act of typing throws up ideas but all it does for others is type jumble. With an active and open mind you will never be short of ideas – indeed you will have more than you will ever be able to use. Study every bit of written material you spot: newspapers, magazines, posters, leaflets, announcements, lists of facts and figures, appeals – anything and everything. Listen to radio and watch television with your idea-finding senses on full alert. And don't be embarrassed about listening to other people when they are talking to each other and paying no attention to you. Eavesdropping with an innocent faraway look on your face can be immensely satisfying! Listen in to other people's conversations in railway carriages or shopping queues or anywhere where people talk. Listen, let your thoughts wander and train them to throw up useful ideas worth working on.

I read a quote by the chairman of a major brewery at their first alcohol-free annual meeting. He revealed that at the previous annual meeting 'members had tried to leave with 156 bottles of wine, whole Stilton cheeses, turkeys and an entire salmon on a silver platter.' Plaintively, he ended, 'I welcome you who are more interested in the company than the food.' I was so tickled by this I just had to find out how much food is 'lost' at conferences and major functions of organisations such as this. The facts and figures provided by leading London hotels letting out banqueting suites and conference dining rooms were a revelation. Wine, turkeys and even a whole salmon, complete with silver platter, were nothing! Quite apart from the dishonesty, how to do people do such a thing? And in my research into this bizarre topic, what astounded me most was the number of apparently-honest folk who laughed, when told, and said, 'Well, it isn't really stealing, is it?' What would magazine readers think of that?

A women's magazine liked the idea of an investigation into how hand gestures differ from nation to nation, sometimes giving inadvertent offence, and other naive ways of insulting people in other countries. On the same tack, a motoring title was interested in a similar piece based on the unofficial signs motorists give each other – and how they may be interpreted differently (sometimes with disastrous effects) in various places.

The woodworking firm of Robert Thompson (1876–1955) of Kilburn, North Yorkshire, adopted a distinctive and much-loved trademark. It was a small mouse which adorns secular and ecclesiastical furniture in more than 700 churches, schools, houses and offices in Britain and abroad, including the pews of the garrison church at Catterick Camp. What a lovely story. It has been written about already, many times, but can you give it a new edge?

Keep your eyes and ears on careers, interests, newspapers, television and radio. The world over, people want ideas to satisfy hunger, thirst (for knowledge as well as food), sex, health, love: think about – anything. Which tools in daily use are not adapted for left-handed folk? More people in this country are born in May than in any other single month, the dis/advantages of owning your own caravan, regularising the date of Easter, more than 5,000 people a year in the UK lose their hearing after swimming, local rags-to-riches stories, house conversions that went wrong, new ways to use spring vegetables, amateur theatre has more devotees than football, why is pigeon racing so popular?

It's just a matter of being on automatic alert: noting all that happens, thinking backwards – and forwards, seeing and hearing through new eyes and ears. What gladdens or saddens, interests or reassures, consoles or explains, intrigues or inspires? To help germination take place ask yourself searching questions: why? who? what? where? when? and how? Twist the questions round too: why didn't? when did? what if? In writing non-fiction all five senses play as crucial a role as they ever do in writing fiction. Someone once said to me, on learning I wrote non-fiction, 'Oh, you're not a proper writer then? You don't have to use your imagination.' I didn't know whether to smile, seethe or pity the speaker: on reflection, I decided the last emotion would be the fairest. In finding ideas to write about, imagination is vital.

Topicality and timing

Submitting to a magazine at the right time often makes the difference between success and rejection.

The business of magazine publishing is highly organised and falls into several clearly defined parts. There is a great deal of work to be done between editorial planning for edition X and the final appearance of edition X on the bookstalls. Magazines take time to assemble before even reaching the printing stage. We've touched on these vital lead times in the last chapter, so here is a reminder:

For an edition to be published at (say) the beginning of May, go back four months to the start of January. This is the month in which the May issue will be planned and articles will be allotted space, along with everything else that will go into the May pages. Every section of planning each issue must work to set timing because the printers, for instance, will almost certainly handle a number of different magazines and each will be booked in for a set period. But the buying, i.e. acceptance of freelance submissions, will already have taken place before this – say during December. So for your article to stand the best chance of appearing in the May edition, from the timing viewpoint alone, it should be on the editor's desk not later than early to mid-December. For Christmas issues your copy (particularly if unsolicited) should be comfortably placed before editors by late June (you can afford to delay a further month or so if not 'going in cold') when some of their December editions will already have been tentatively laid out.

It is essential to observe this gap between the conception of a particular issue and its eventual publication, and if you're hoping to sell your copy for a special edition, for instance at the time of the Olympic Games or a Royal event, be sure to give yourself an extra few weeks on top of the magazine's usual lead time. Despite all advice you may find lead time varies between publications and that even those published monthly, for example, work to varying schedules. In general consider a well-established monthly to have a lead time of at least four months, probably six and possibly eight. Lead times are reduced for weekly periodicals but the same principle obtains – and for all titles the lead time can be ascertained by a simple enquiry.

Have 'timed' copy ready for anything that definitely will happen or is most likely to happen. Whether it be a special anniversary or a royal death you can have done all the work and be ready to submit your copy while other writers are still thinking about how to collect the facts. A steady stream of articles is sent by hopeful writers on famous anniversaries and at times of seasonal celebration, so if you plan to join the throng you must think of an unusual aspect of the subject and give it something very special to make an anniversary-weary editor feel life is still worth living.

Many magazines publish regular nostalgia pieces with such titles as 'Fifty years ago' or 'This month in (then follows a particular year)'. These are satisfactory pieces to write and if you have access to a store of early records or old editions of the magazine itself you can easily write short items on a wide variety of themes to please everyone.

Regular events and anniversaries are good triggers for topical articles but the link between the date (or person, or event) must be strong for your article to stand a chance. Ask yourself 'Why should an editor want this now?' and 'Why should he buy my article rather than someone else's about this topic?' If you can't find good answers to both questions he probably won't.

What do you know?

Your own experience of life is a valuable source of ideas with the advantage you will certainly be able to write with authority. Give yourself the exercise of reflecting on what you did yesterday and make a list of a dozen ideas your activities suggested. For instance, it may be impossible to find the recipe for a particular dish currently popular with children, so you assembled the ingredients and wrote out the cooking instructions in simple terms. With a picture of the finished product this could find a ready audience of grateful mums in the right magazine. Perhaps your bike broke down and you fixed it; other bikers face this problem and many don't know how to fix it. Your friends running small businesses may provide you with ideas by their very enterprise. Two sisters, aged 40+, in my village were facing early retirement, which neither wanted, and set up in business cleaning out people's wheelie bins after the council emptied them every week. Clad in hygienic face masks, red bobble hats and white boiler-suits, they wielded high pressure hoses as if born to the job – and many were the encouraging smiles received from grateful customers when 'Bill & Ben, the wheelie-clean men' doffed their masks and hats. That made such a good story for a local magazine the editor was pleased to be giving the wheelie-clean 'men' free publicity, and me a good fee. Naturally I didn't let it rest there as this was certainly a story for a larger audience ...

Women's magazines often want 'What happened to me' stories – frequently accompanied by pictures. And unusual but true stories are always popular. I talked to a woman whose three-year old daughter had been marooned in a burning building. As she and her husband were held back by firemen they (and other people on the ground) saw a young woman appear at an upstairs window. She shouted to the firemen and threw down the child – who was caught uninjured. The parents swore there was nobody else in the house at the time, that they had never seen the young woman before and had no idea how she came to be in their house to save their daughter's life. In due course the firemen put out the fire. They found no body but among the burned timbers of the child's bedroom they did find a gold bracelet which they returned to the child's parents. They had never seen it before. This was, of course, a true story but not until it was published in a women's magazine was the mother able to – I can't say 'finish it' so much as 'add another twist to it'. The week after publication a young man identified the bracelet. He had given it to his girlfriend soon after she discovered she would never be able to bear a child but she had scorned it and walked out on him. He had not seen her since and had assumed she had left the neighbourhood.

Does an unfinished story intrigue you as it does me? I checked all the authorities but could find no trace of any girl reported missing and as far as I can discover there has been no further development of the story.

As the chapter on market study will remind you, be careful when writing about your own affairs. There are magazines welcoming nostalgia or personal opinions but writing about something too close to your heart in a market not wanting either will kill your story. Another risk in writing about what you know (advice regularly offered to beginners without this warning) is that being so close to your subject you may find it hard or even impossible to explain it to readers new to the subject. Writers of computer manuals regularly fall into this trap: many a manual designed for newcomers to computing is nigh incomprehensible until a friend has explained it in non-technical terms – and then you understand it and barely need the manual anyway. So be careful you don't assume readers have as much knowledge of your pet subject as you have – or veer too far the other way and think their ignorance of it makes them idiots.

In truth everything you have ever known or thought or felt or witnessed or heard or read or wanted or feared or dreamed about (or eaten, suffered, enjoyed – the list is endless) is material in which ideas are found. A fertile imagination responds well to exercise and soon you'll find you have more than enough to write about – of the right sort.

Ideas from ads and pix

Advertisements and pictures (ads and pix, as journalists call them) provide useful source material for idea-hunters. To hit the nail right on the head, in terms of what the ad is trying to sell, is what advertising copy-writers are paid for. The most successful ads incorporate a good idea just as do the most successful articles. Viewers are also magazine readers so clever advertisers are quick to exploit what appeals to public imagination.

Look at pictures in a new light: not only advertising pix but also others in public places, on magazine or newspaper pages, on television – anywhere and everywhere. Browsing on newsagents' shelves isn't only useful when you're looking for markets to write for; a quick flip through published copies of those potential markets can prove valuable in giving you ideas about what to write. Sometimes it can also surprise you. Finding a feature on the very topic you have in the back of your mind may not be welcome but at least it will save you time and effort in what would probably have been wasted research for that market.

An endless supply

Look at any dictionary of dates and you'll be bursting with ideas before reaching the second page. Here are anniversaries by the thousand covering events in countless spheres: entertainment, politics, royalty, shipwrecks, music, battles – anything you care to name will have anniversaries editors will buy. Opened at random *Chamber's Dictionary of Dates* tells me 26 December 1997 will be the fortieth anniversary of the world's first charity walk. It took place along the Icknield Way, in aid of the World Refugee Fund. In August 1936 Elizabeth Cowell made her debut at Alexandra Palace in Muswell Hill, North London as the first woman television announcer. Oliver Cromwell declared Britain a Commonwealth and abolished the Monarchy in March 1649.

Remember the schoolboy who thought history began with William the Conqueror and ended with Queen Victoria? Nobody explained to him that history is what happens today – looked at tomorrow. Events in the recent past are always popular in small localities so articles about local history often sell well in magazines with an area or limited circulation. Let an editor receive an article he knows will evoke responses of 'Ah yes, do you remember ...?' from his readers and all else being equal he'll probably buy it.

If you like looking at the past to make an article for the future, buy a good book of dates, scan the pages of any encyclopaedia or study material published in the area. Inspiration won't be long in coming.

To start you off ...

Adopt the habit of idea-thinking everywhere you go and with everything you do. The frogspawn in my pond develops into hundreds of tadpoles many of which do not survive into baby let alone adult frogs. Idea-germination is similarly prolific and at first may seem equally wasteful, but I've often found a tadpole stored away in a forgotten corner of my mind will develop later and become quite a handy frog. A wise man makes more opportunities than he finds (according to Francis Bacon) and mentally nothing is ever wasted. Take a look at these, for instance:

1 Mnemonics have been one of my hobbies for many years and I have written many articles on this theme. They intrigue a lot of other people and the more I write about them the more I collect as readers send me their favourites. This is an example of choosing popular subjects to write about – or at least subjects that fall into the 'light amusement' category. Many readers will remember:

Willy Willy Harry Ste
Harry, Dick John Harry III
One two three Neds, Richard II
Henry IV, V, VI – then who?[1]

but not so well-known (and therefore seized upon by enthusiasts) is the order in which Henry VIII married his wives:

Catherine of Aragon stole a jar of tarragon.
'It's the last in the bin,' she told Anne Boleyn.
'Give me more!' begged Jane Seymour.
Which made Anne of Cleeves spill some on her sleeves.
'Not for me! I'm a coward!' said Catherine Howard.
But Catherine Parr drank the rest of the jar.

[1] you do know the rest ... er, don't you?

or (just to show not all mnemonics have royal connections):

Bless My Dear Aunt Sally[2]

2 Shopping: does competition always help the customer? How the big stores team up on prices – on the quiet. And how they spy on each other to see who's letting the others down.

3 'Cyril came to stay for a month' told the story of a tiny grey squirrel found cowering in a hedge and how we fed him from a baby's bottle until he was big and fit enough to be released into the wild.

4 Pantomime was never invented – it just grew. This is a fascinating story, particularly at the right time of year.

5 A collection of press misprints made hilarious reading in a popular weekly magazine:

   The survey records there are 10,638 people sharing an outside toilet.
   Photographer will shoot children for Christmas.
   A body was found in a burnt out hen house on Saturday but police do not suspect foul play.

Here are a few of my personal collection of headlines:

   MINERS REFUSE TO WORK AFTER DEATH
   20 YEAR FRIENDSHIP ENDS AT ALTAR
   IRAQI HEAD SEEKS ARMS
   DRUNK GETS SIX MONTHS IN VIOLIN CASE
   JUDGE TO RULE ON NUDE BEACH

and seen at the time of argument over the ordination of women in the Church of England:

   DO YOU WANT A WOMAN VICAR?

6 Listening to a relative's fight to help a family in Mexico gave me the idea for an article about how one small community there copes with trouble.

7 The well-loved words about death by Canon Scott Holland can bring comfort to readers of widely different publications: Death is nothing at all ... I have only slipped away into the next room ... Although we long to help the bereaved, death is still a topic few of us can write about. Can you?

---

[2] the order of numerical or algebraic expression: brackets, multiplication, division, addition and subtraction.

Anyone could fill this book with lists of ideas; maybe some of the above will light a spark in your head, giving birth to an original idea. For nobody else's ideas will be as valuable to you as those you think up for yourself – because they will be yours.

Remember, the first glimmering of a general idea is often vague and insubstantial – until it gives way to the particular one unique to you. If you feel yourself adrift in an idea-empty sea or an ocean of floating images that don't interconnect, set yourself the task of listing five ideas you think you could write about and do it now. Carry your list about with you and study it constantly until you decide which single idea is going to be the first to have your full attention.

Changing and developing ideas

Make many articles out of a single idea. One day I watched a girl in a hairdresser's salon sweeping up bits of hair that had been cut from customers' heads. I wondered how much human hair was thrown away every day throughout the world and how far it would stretch were it all joined together in a single thread. Idle musing? Perhaps. But it led to a string (sic) of articles in a variety of magazines on the following themes:

1 Hair care and cleanliness in the eighteenth century. (Some of the facts I uncovered were pretty hair-*raising*)

2 Why men make top hairdressers for women.

3 Your mirror image: what does it reveal? (Facts and figs about left and right handedness)

4 Hair today, why gone tomorrow? (What to do with hair we throw away. Suggestions ranged from mixing it with tarmac for absorbing rain on roads to composting it into a new thatching material vying with straw for the 'natural' epithet)

5 Your hair is what you eat. (A diet-for-health piece)

6 Models never complain. (About dressing the hair of dummies in museums etc)

Often digging into how you are going to deal with a particular idea throws up what strikes you as a better one. If this happens (as if frequently does to me) be glad that you're getting two or even more ideas from one and put aside the one(s) you don't immediately start working on. There is no failure in changing your mind about what you are going to write as long it only happens in private. If you are going to present your ideas rather than the finished article to an editor you must be quite sure there is no changing your mind after he's approved it or agreed you should go ahead with the project.

If one good idea leads to another, as it certainly does, make sure you don't spend all your time generating ideas, invaluable as they are. Before too long you must make a clear decision about which one you're going to develop next. Only you have access to those revolving inside your head – and for you they will be the best.

Well travelled words

Travel is a field which demands specialist attention and it is not always as easy as it sounds. Writing articles about your holidays, where you've been, what you've done and seen, interesting people you've met, and so on, can make very worthwhile copy and often sells well. I know several freelance writers who regularly recoup all they spend on holidays by writing about them. Some go further and make a point of lining up possible markets whenever they travel anywhere – on business, for family reasons or for their own relaxation. A large number of magazines publish copy about travel for readers who simply want to know about places they've heard of or read about and might like to see for themselves. Magazine-wise they are potential tourists rather than travellers.

Wherever we writers go, within these shores or overseas, we can always take an unusual viewpoint, find a fascinating person, reveal little-known information or offer practical advice to others following in our footsteps. A place that is familiar to you, because you've been there before, will be excitingly original for countless readers who haven't. It's your job as a 'tourist' writer to give them a taste for it. Tempt them with the flavour, encourage them with descriptive and imaginative language and resolve their doubts with solid facts and figures about getting there, details of where they can stay, the currency, any paperwork or special health regulations involved and anything else they would want to ask if you were telling them of your experiences face to face.

Being a 'travel writer' is rather different, particularly in the eyes of most glossy publications. Those existing solely as travel rather than general or other-topic magazines frequently complain at receiving too many mundane accounts of people's holidays. Their editors seldom accept unsolicited copy and all work is either directly commissioned or at least arranged after detailed consultation. For the cover prices they charge, the quality of the advertisements they attract and the 'travel professionalism' their readers expect, only the best will do. With high standards to maintain they will even reject copy already invited (which is not the same as commissioned) if it fails to evoke in readers the essential 'feeling' of the place visited. Here again, study of the market is particularly important as the magazines wanting travel articles vary greatly in their levels of sophistication.

A most useful book on the subject is: *Writing about Travel* by Morag Campbell, A & C Black. The author was for many years editor of *Signature*, the Diners Club magazine, which involved the commissioning of travel articles. Having travelled the world and contributed travel articles to countless publications she includes every aspect of the job. £5.95.

Borrow, copy or steal?

It is horribly easy to think up an idea, work on it in your head and even on paper, convince yourself it has not been done before – and find you are wrong. So where do borrowing, copying or even stealing begin and end?

Some years ago a well-known women's magazine ran a competition inviting its readers to write a short story. Thousands of entries were received and among those short-listed for further consideration one struck the judging panel as particularly clever. It was about a woman who called the police and told them she had found her husband dead in the house when she returned home. Plainly he had been hit on the head with a blunt instrument. While the police searched the house for further clues, the victim's wife cooked them a succulent joint of roast lamb, which they ate with relish. The story, titled *Consuming Evidence*, was an obvious winner and was awarded first prize.

But when it was duly published in the magazine a memory stirred in the head of someone who recalled reading something very similar, called *Lamb to the Slaughter*, in a book of short stories by the well-known author Roald Dahl. A complaint was made to the magazine and was upheld. In substance and plot, if not in the quality of writing, it was the same story.

The final irony, as if to emphasise to the author the awful consequences of plagiarism, be it innocent or flagrant, lay in the title of the 'winning' story. A zealous sub-editor on the magazine had thought the author's choice could be improved and had replaced *Consuming Evidence* with – yes, you've guessed it – *Lamb to the Slaughter.*

No matter what the *real* story behind this one, and ignoring whether the hapless author was guilty of plagiarism or was merely the victim of a memory-trick that catches out most of us, i.e. reading something somewhere, forgetting we have done so, and thinking we have invented it when it surfaces in our minds months or even years later, the result was the same: shame and embarrassment for everyone concerned. We can only do our best to be original in all our thinking as well as in our writing.

On the principle that there is nothing new in the universe, decide to write about, for instance, pollution in Britain and of course you won't be the first person to do so. But you are not guilty of borrowing, copying or stealing someone else's idea. What matters is the imagination and enthusiasm the idea plants in your head, coupled with your unique way of writing about it. The ideas in a previous section may be no help to you because they ignite no spark; if that is so, it is because they are not your ideas. Use other people's to find your own, to set you reflecting, contrasting, developing and generally giving your imagination room to expand in the way only you can. When I first understood what pundits meant by such 'lateral thinking' I realised I had been doing it instinctively all my life. Ideas float about by the million but the best for you are fed by a natural individuality that will show through the written words and breathe life into your work.

Testing ideas

To test ideas objectively, let them lie fallow for a while. When you look at them again you will no longer be blinded by what seemed a brilliant conception and can ask yourself some rigorous questions. The first – will this idea be of sufficient interest to editors and readers? – will be answered by detailed market study (see Chapter 3) but even before that you must ask 'Do I have or can I obtain all the information I'm going to need to develop the idea?' Only if the answer is 'Yes' can you go ahead with any degree of hope (I almost said 'confidence' but that might be a little too optimistic at this stage of the article-planning process).

Later in this book you will find details of how to set about the research work required to put backbone and credibility into articles. It is a comfort to know experts in research have gone before us and can put us on the right track in that vital aspect of writing.

Knowing or assembling facts and figures needed for the task is one thing: assessing whether you have enough may be quite another. Everything we write is more convincing when we know a great deal more 'behind the scenes' than we need to reveal to the reader. Such extra knowledge adds a certain authority and reliability to our work which reassures the reader that we really do know what we're writing about.

So an idea must be followed by the initial finding of at least the important facts to support it before a judgement can be made about its viability. Never fall into the error of trying to clothe an idea, particularly what might otherwise have been a good one, in costume so scanty it won't keep out cold editorial condemnation. Trying to spread the sparse covering further than it will go only leads what's underneath to a quicker death.

A different test to subject your ideas to concerns pictures. Will the resultant article(s) need them, or be more likely to sell with them? Chapter 10: Pix deals with this aspect of article-submission but before you begin writing you need to answer 'Will I need pix?' And if the answer is 'Yes' can you acquire them?

An ideas file

When your head is crammed with ideas and you are surrounded by scrappy notes on bits of paper it is time to sort them into files. Mine are usually concertina-type cardboard files in which I store items of idea-generating information usually in the form of clips and cuttings I find here and there. As you look out for ideas you should also watch for cuttings: bits out of newspapers or magazines you might find useful. Be sure to check what your cuttings tell you (could the writer be wrong?) and always date them.

Most writers carry notepads all the time. Some paper, a pen and a little pair of folding scissors can work wonders for your storage files. (I hope my dentist isn't reading this but I'm always glad to be left alone in the waiting room as he has a lively supply of magazines on the table ...) Look upon ideas as not only necessary to work on now, but also as your stock in trade for a rainy day in the future.

I confess I've often found it easier to write about a fixed subject than pluck one out of the air. If an editor indicates he wants an article about David Knopfler or why we are not shoulder-deep in non-biodegradable ballpoint pens you may breathe a sign of relief that the topic itself indicates the route you must follow to complete the task. There will be no problem of finding an idea or worrying about whether you can or can't support it with all the necessary facts and figures. Meanwhile you'll have a pleasant surprise the next time you glance at the bulging ideas file you are constantly adding to. With all those ideas of your own jostling for your attention, idea-finding will never be a problem again.

3
Markets

If you remember the world is full of people just like you and me it is not difficult to find markets – for what we are really studying is not magazines but readers. There are several well-established market guides (listed at the end of this chapter) and between them they cover a huge number of consumer titles, most of which are wide open to freelance contributions. They are so-called because they are 'consumed', i.e. bought, in quantity at regular intervals by the general public. In other spheres such as the food business, marketing men refer to items as 'fmcg' – fast-moving consumer goods.

Editors are not only delighted to receive publishable material in their daily postbags, they actually rely on it. There are magazines wanting us as badly as we want them but many freelance writers ignore three quarters of the available markets because they do not know they exist. For example, there are more than 2,000 small magazines and journals that do not carry advertising and may never reach the pages of published guides.

Target magazines

With magazines launched (and folding) almost every week a rough estimate of the number publishing freelance material at any one time can only be approximate; ten thousand would not be a wild guess. Among this super-abundance of magazines to contribute to let's take a look at the main publishers of the big consumer titles: sorting-by-ownership is a logical and valuable way of grouping magazines together.

Circulation proclaims success as nothing else can; glossy covers, stunning publicity, brilliant contents, dedicated editorial work and everything else that goes into a magazine count for nought if the number of copies sold is insufficient to support the cost of production. Sales are measured by the Audit Bureau of Circulation which reports its findings every six months.

These are the current leaders with their circulation figures:

Reader's Digest	1,673,000
What's On TV	1,633,000
Take a Break	1,508,000
Radio Times	1,463,000
TV Times	1,015,000

It can be no coincidence that periodicals with a television theme regularly feature at the top of the list. BBC Publishing has the unique advantage over other publishers in being able to support its titles with television and radio programmes about food, gardening, antiques, etc. Some major publishers are diversifying into areas other than print: EMAP (East Midlands Allied Press) is also a major commercial radio operator and the Anglo-Dutch merger of Reed Elsevier, Britain's largest periodical publisher employing over 25,000 people, has extensive interests in medical, legal and on-line publishing.

The famous five from IPC (*Woman's Weekly*, *Woman's Own*, *Woman*, *Woman's Realm* and *Woman and Home*) come in the top thirty titles. The other leading publishers are in strong competition. Argus Press concentrates on hobby magazines such as *Aeromodeller*, *Model Boats*, *Woodworker* and *Popular Crafts*; Bauer produce *Take a Break*, *Bella*, and *TV Quick*; Benn Business Publishing (owned by Miller Freeman, formerly Morgan-Grampian) list *Music Week*, *Studio Sound* and *Chemist & Druggist* among their 70+ titles; and up-market *House & Garden*, *Vogue* and *Brides* come from Conde Nast Publications.

The publishing giant EMAP publishes some 90 titles in two magazine divisions, business and consumer; the latter is sub-divided into seven editorial offices covering:

bikes/cars
computers/games
gardens/cameras/rail
health/parenting/lifestyle
music/entertainment
sport/wildlife
women.

IPC Magazines (the UK's most prolific periodical publisher and a subsidiary of Reed Elsevier) floods the bookstalls with – among others – weeklies *Amateur Photographer*, *Angler's Mail* and *Amateur Gardening*, and monthlies *Practical Parenting*, *Marie Claire*, *Your Garden* and *Classic Cars*. Link House, the National Magazine

Company and D. C. Thomson and Co. are just three more of the companies at the forefront of periodical publishing.

Hidden away . . .

In a separate category, for assessment purposes, with circulation figures seldom recorded by the Audit Bureau of Circulation, lie the large number of trade and business magazines. Their success is measured by the value of the display advertising carried on their pages although some may be subsidised to a degree. From the writer's point of view there is virtually no difference between studying the pages of trade or business titles and poring over consumer magazines: if either want freelance contributors, that's the only spur we need. There's just one point about that word 'virtually'; because trade or business magazines are less obvious targets freelance writers submitting to their pages often face little competition.

The cost of advertising in the pages of a magazine are (or should be) directly related to what it is likely to pay freelance contributors. Fees charged by magazines for companies wanting to buy space in which to publicise their wares, be they large corporate business or small private enterprises, are grouped in bands.

Here is a selection of titles in relevant bands at current page rates; it is important to remember the latter may vary outside these limits (in either direction) and are constantly changing:

Group A: £5,000+ (which is more than doubled by the first four for a colour page): *Woman, Woman's Own, Good Housekeeping, Take a Break, Computer Weekly, Bella, Family Circle, Elle* and *Country Living.*

Group B: £3,000 – £5,000: *Mother & Baby, Yours, PC User, Today, Marie Claire, Choice* and *New Scientist.*

Group C: £1,500 – £3,000: *Country Life, Parents, Accountancy, Wedding and Home, Health Service Journal* and *The Universe.*

Group D: £500 – £1,500: *The Lady, Caterer & Hotelkeeper, Practical Photography, Irish World* and *Everywoman.*

Group E: under £500 or carrying no advertising at all: ethnic and small circulation titles (which often pay low or no fees to freelances).

You will find a more detailed assessment of how much you may expect to be paid in relation to these advertising bands in Chapter 11.

Nobody's forgotten

Every industry, profession and occupation has its own publication – and sometimes more than one. There are an estimated 6,000 separate titles, including those issued by commercial companies, building societies and banks, which reflect the interests of potential readers. The established market guides offer details of many trade titles. Some might be 'controlled' which means contributions are mostly written by 'insiders' but don't let that deter you. If you write what the editor wants space will always be found, regardless of who you are. The reason is not hard to find: behind the professional or business people are ordinary folk who have other interests besides their jobs. They want to enjoy their spare time and at work or at play they (like everyone else) often appreciate a touch of humour; these magazines are not exclusively devoted to 'business' matters.

So you don't have to be a builder to sell to a magazine for builders any more than you have to be Jewish to write for a Jewish magazine or a computer expert to sell to the computer market. I am not a builder, Jewish or a computer expert but I have sold to all three types of periodical. I have also sold countless articles to the medical press over the years, all written from my viewpoint of being the only non-medical member of a large and otherwise entirely-medical family. Yes, the background for this copy came naturally to me so it was (and is) a matter of 'writing about what you know'. But for some time I also wrote a light-hearted column for a publication read by engineers working in heating and ventilation about which I know nothing at all. In the latter case much of my copy centred round comic situations resulting from customers' lack of knowledge of the trade. I suspect my own genuine ignorance was more of a help than a hindrance in selling my work. Even knowing nothing can sometimes be useful!

Supermarkets, stores, insurance companies, travel firms and motor manufacturers – most will have their own publications but where do you find these in-house magazines, especially if you are not part of a business or company issuing one and do not know anyone who is? You could ask for information from your local public library or contact the Department of Trade and Industry's Companies Division (1 Victoria Street, London SW1H 0ET) or the British Library's Business Information Service. Perhaps the most practical way to find a personal opening is to talk to someone working in any capacity for a large organisation or company. He (or she) will know of any in-house publication and, with luck, provide you with a few recent issues. These magazines exist for two main purposes: to keep employees informed about what the company or organisation is doing and to strengthen unity and loyalty within it. For the observant freelance reading between the lines there are often opportunities for articles to inform, interest or entertain readers on topics quite apart from the organisation's mainstream occupation.

Whichever category your selected target titles falls into you can be encouraged by the proliferation of small-interest titles with greater prospects of success in our increasingly fragmented society. Gone are the days when we (as readers) were classified *en masse* solely by age, gender, income, education and so on. The spread and sophistication of desktop publishing has reduced costs to such an extent that even small markets can run at a profit.

Several may, for example, be magazines covering the interests of specialist groups, publications restricted to members of particular groups or societies, hobby titles published by and for enthusiasts, or small press productions and titles published at irregular intervals, perhaps only for particular purposes. Almost all rely on freelance material. They range from *Areopagus* (a quarterly publishing articles and smaller pieces in Winchester) to *TEMS NEWS*, a newsy and topical periodical devoted to UFOs, crytozoology and fortean phenomena, with a huge range of titles covering every conceivable interest in between.

Potential contributors to small press periodicals should remember their fragility and always make the first move an enquiry about the title's state of health. And maybe you will learn more than how to write for magazines if you study Mencap's monthly newspaper; the editor is currently looking for writers who can attend an event – an interview, or a show, perhaps – with folk with learning disabilities and then help them write items for the magazine.

Such flexibility enables minority-interest groups to be viable in publishing terms, offering yet more scope for freelance writers. They maintain a special place in writers' affections and the topics they cover vary enormously. To discover more you might like to contact the Small Press Group, BM Bozo, London WC1N 3XX.

Sorting by appeal

Periodicals fall into specific categories according to the likes and tastes of readers they are designed to capture so in talking about types of magazines we are really referring to the types of readers who (without realising it) dictate the content, price, cover, advertisements and editorial slant of every title in the market place.

This is a broad selection of the types available:

animals, birds & fish	literary & fiction
art & antiques	men's interests
business & finance	motoring
buying & selling	music & hi-fi
children & young people	outdoor activities
computers & on-line	photography
county & regional	puzzles & crosswords
current & world affairs	sports
electronics	teenage & pop
entertainment	trade & professional
hobbies & pastimes	transport
home & garden	travel
international	women's interests

'General interest' titles represent a large and difficult-to-categorise section of the magazine world. In the trade it is the term used to describe periodicals that appeal to a wide variety of readers who themselves cannot be readily classified. Religion, for instance, and health and humour are of interest to people of all levels of intelligence and taste although they may be of particular appeal to many folk. In the general interest category you will find magazines such as *Astronomy Now* and *Reader's Digest* with each classified or general interest type embracing widely varying titles. For example, 'children & young people' is broken down into more than 400 (yes, four hundred) separate publications. The number of titles devoted to any one theme can be bewildering. 'Motoring' supports many different publications, as do 'music' and 'cookery'. In fact it is hard to think of a single topic not subdivided into a whole range of titles, so great is the variety and range of readers' interests.

They know best

People who depend on it for a living – the publishing companies – know exactly what they're doing in market study and there is much we can learn from them. Every issue of every magazine reveals telltale signs of how the market-researchers have done their work. Why do some titles succeed and others fail? What makes people buy one rather than another one in competition with it? Is the 'masthead' (the title of the magazine usually splashed across the top of the front cover) clear and bright? Is there a catchy title slogan? Is the magazine's appeal obvious? A publication without a clearly defined target is doomed to failure. (But even if it folds you may be able to snatch profit out of disaster: keeping tabs on which editors have gone where and taken personal likes and dislikes to new markets can be valuable market study.)

As magazine publishers and editors plan their target reader-ship very carefully indeed before launching expensive new titles, they consider the average reader for the age group they hope to reach. So when you know the age or approximate age of a maga-zine's readers you will have the first overall idea of the sort of people the magazine is hoping to attract. Given an age range of, say, 18 – 24 the average age aimed at would be 21 but great care would be taken not to limit or even concentrate the title's appeal to those aged 21. There is no profit in gaining half a dozen new readers by appealing to their exact age group and losing six others by ignoring theirs. If you cannot discover the average reader-age of a particular title despite research and your closest market study, simply contact the magazine and ask.

Getting down to it

Market study is rather like trying to unbake a cake. There are all the ingredients, mixed to perfection by an expert; to discover the recipe the cake must be unbaked, i.e. reduced to its constituent parts. But doing that will only reveal the ingredients of that particular cake. And here our allegory ends: many cakes are baked to a single recipe, as we all know, but no periodicals are the same week after week or month after month.

Research into the market guides listed in this chapter is a beginning and will provide outline information about maga-zines, but true market study means studying the magazines themselves. There is no substitute for purposeful, thorough and organised appraisal of the contents of your potential market over a period of time. For monthly magazines a study of at least six issues is advisable, including the most recent, and paying close attention to at least ten editions of a weekly magazine is likely to yield the best results. Magazines published as part of the leading newspapers offer a hard-to-enter but well-paid opportunity. The *Sunday Telegraph*, for example, demands 'nothing but the very best, intelligent writing' for its magazine.

When we've found the magazines we want to write for (or think we want to write for, as further acquaintance with them might make us change our minds), how do we set about the actual study? To do it at all is important, not so each of us may discover exactly what everyone else studying them discovers, but in order to bring that extra personal impression to our minds – so we don't all emerge with identical opinions and subsequently write articles lacking originality. That is also why market study has no hard-and-fast rules but what I can only call guidelines to be bent and stretched to suit you, as an individual writer. You may have read conflicting advice about the whole matter. You may even have heard some writers boast they never bother with it at all; have you also heard about their level of success or failure compared to the number of scripts they submit to editors?

So here are some guidelines, beset with provisos and cautions and let-outs as all such precepts must be when they attempt to govern anything as creative and character-driven as writing:

1 discover what magazines exist for readers who share or might share interest in your chosen topic;

2 buy, beg or borrow as many different magazines on the topic as you can;

3 study them analytically as a writer as well as a reader for insight into editorial aims;

4 make your choice of market (or markets) and stick to your decision – while not closing your mind to future articles along similar or allied lines;

5 keep note of any new ideas born of studying the magazine(s) and set them aside for future development.

There are tutors who advise scrupulous dissection of every word, analysing its place, purpose and effectiveness until the whole magazine is reduced to a mass of tangled statistics. I fear this is more like character assassination than market study and kills the very goose I hope is going to nurse my golden egg. And to describe a magazine as having character is a valid assessment of what makes it what it is, just as each of us has a personality different from that of anyone else. Discerning the individual personality of your chosen magazine can spell the difference between success and failure. Titles for dog owners, for instance, vary in their basic policies: one will favour the professional breeder while another is aimed at the ordinary dog owner who only wants practical help in bringing up the family dog.

Of course sensible analysis is important. Take a sheet of paper and write down the number of pages of your chosen market, noting what proportion of them is given to advertising, editorial matter (that's everything written in-house by the editor or staff) and other copy. The last may or may not be written by freelances and regular examination of consecutive issues will often reveal whether particular items are, or were, freelance 'spaces'. Don't be downcast if you cannot at first differentiate between freelance and non-freelance material; this is a skill that greatly improves with practice.

List the published articles and classify them according to type, appeal, length, impact (especially of the opening paragraph) and closing 'feel'. Note the price and frequency of publication, both of which give an immediate indication of the readers who are its target. Observe the quality of the paper, the effectiveness of layout and the calibre of the illustrations. All these help to give you a picture of the average reader. (If there are pictures and you want to submit some with your copy in due course, see the relevant chapter later in this book.)

Articles written in the first-person will almost certainly be freelance, as will anything temporarily out of the usual style for the magazine you are studying. Assuming they have the space and that company policy allows them a degree of flexibility, editors seldom observe rigid terms in how much freelance material they buy. If offered just what they want they eagerly bend any preconceived plans for a particular issue not already advanced beyond the 'no-change' stage. So when your market study tells you magazine X devotes, say, 60% of its content to freelance material and most of that seems to be filled with regular or specialist columns, don't abandon any hopes you may have of submitting to it. If you write what the editor wants, space will always be found. Perhaps that last sentence sums up all we writers need to know.

Observe the style and structure of the magazine's language and how it treats its readers. Are they spoken to cheerfully, with triviality, as serious-minded thinkers, as if their main concerns are domestic, adventurous, romantic, creative – or how? Is the language used appropriate for immature youngsters, clearly for folk with some experience in the topic the magazine deals with or is there a mixture of styles? Picture the very readers the magazine is trying to reach and if possible think of someone you know who might be one.

There is an army of PROs (Public Relations Officers) waiting to help you. Each is actually waiting to help the people who pay the wages, which will be the publishing company promoting the magazine, but they can be of great value to writers. Ask for statistics of the readership of your chosen magazine, the launch plans (if it is new or about to be launched) and any other relevant material they care to supply. You never know what they might hand out and the more useful information you assemble the better.

It is always possible to write and ask for back numbers of the title(s) you are studying (with an offer to pay for them and a stamped self-addressed envelope of adequate size) but editorial offices are busy places, your request may not be directed to the appropriate person and you may not receive what you want.

The most valuable advice anyone can offer in the business of market study is this: get to 'know' the readers as well as you know your friends. Then you will instinctively understand what they do and do not want. And once you understand, you know exactly what to write. When your copy is published you'll get no help from nods of agreement, frowns, 'Ah, this is just what I want,' or even 'Rubbish!' as your article is thrown down in disgust. You have to judge (or do your best to judge, which is really the most any of us can do) how readers' minds work.

That is what communication is all about in every type of writing: understanding what goes on in other people's heads and knowing how to get something out of yours into theirs.

Look after women

There are still some special categories that deserve particular marketing attention and one covers the huge number of magazines for and about women.

Although you may not particularly want to write for women (at the moment, at least) so overwhelming is the concentration of magazines geared to their interests that you would be distancing yourself from a large and potentially lucrative section of the overall market were you to ignore it. Women buy over 80% of all titles of all types and 'women's interest' titles sell in greater quantities than do those in any other single section of the market. Most importantly for us, editors of these magazines buy a higher proportion of what they print from freelances than do editors of other magazines. No wonder the 'women's interest' titles are almost worth a book in themselves.

The high circulation figures of the leading magazines for women reflect their constant popularity. These (in round figures) are the current bestsellers:

Bella	981,000
Woman	812,000
Woman's Weekly	798,000
Woman's Own	795,000
Prima	618,000
Best	564,000
Chat	541,000
Good Housekeeping	518,000
People's Friend	479,000
Cosmopolitan	460,000
Woman & Home	435,000
Marie Claire	430,000
My Weekly	423,000

The Lady, born 1885 and the oldest surviving magazine for women, currently sells 66,000 copies a week.

Study women's magazines and you'll quickly see how widely they vary and yet how they share attributes. Apart from appearing weekly or fortnightly (and occasionally at less frequent intervals) at varying prices, the feeling of nearly all – in their different ways – is uplifting. The monthlies usually include more in-depth articles than their weekly counterparts simply because there is a longer time between editions in which to get everything done. Usually, if appropriate to the readership, there will be glossy illustrations, a luxurious tone and a relaxed impression of quality. On the whole the doors of these magazines are closely guarded by writers 'in the know' and it is difficult for newcomers to break into their pages, in fact often impossible without prior contact with the editor. But, as with every publication at every level, those writing for its pages now were at one time unknown ...

The many weeklies for women present less experienced free-lances with countless opportunities. Of course, close study of what is required is essential but always remember, particularly at this vibrant but cut-throat level of competing titles, that what you see in the latest issue is what they decided to publish about six weeks ago. Remember those vital lead times which apply to all periodicals and which, if ignored, can consign to oblivion the brain-child on which you've lavished tender loving care for days or weeks.

The grey market

Another increasingly important category is what is sometimes referred to as the 'grey' market: titles for readers (of both sexes) over fifty. One even states its intended readership is 'the over-40s' and features copy on scuba-diving, property, out-of-the-ordinary activity holidays and investment advice. Times have changed and continue to do so when we're not always looking: read some of these 'grey' titles and you might have a surprise!

Apparent 'outsiders'

It profits freelances to make a special study of magazines outside the ordinary run of those displayed on bookstalls and publicised in market guides. And it pays to study the cover price. This is generally split three ways: the retailer takes 25%, 15% goes to the wholesaler and the publisher takes the lion's share of 60%. But in some cases there isn't a cover price. While the majority of magazines depend on them to boost advertising revenue a few are apparently freely given away. You can find them on aeroplanes, InterCity trains, outside Underground stations, in banks and building societies, estate agents' offices, supermarkets, hotel bedrooms and in numerous other places.

Offering the public an apparent something-for-nothing is not as foolish as it might seem. Psychologically the readers are pleased with the magazine before even opening it. The contents, regardless of what they might be, are greeted with positive acceptance because they are free; readers are not resentful at having wasted good money should an article fail to please, and if they approve of or delight in another they can bask in a self-satisfied glow of having got it for nothing.

From the publisher's point of view there are advantages to offset the obvious disadvantage of having no income from sales. Give away 10,000 copies of a magazine and you will have advertisers flocking to buy space in your pages. You can also aim at a carefully-defined target readership more easily than can your larger paid-for rivals who (despite costly and intensive research) can't avoid missing the bull's-eye and wasting a proportion of their effort and money.

Magazines received by post are also among the 'outsiders'. A large number are bought by prepaid subscription as well as being sold through the usual retail channels but others are available only (or mainly) by subscription, sometimes with enormous success. *Reader's Digest*, for instance, credited with being the highest circulation periodical in the world is sold almost entirely by prepaid subscription. More and more titles on visible sale in this country now also carry invitations to readers to 'take out a regular subscription', often coupled with the offer of tempting goodies. Readers might need sweetening at the prospect of paying for a twelve month or 52 week period in one dollop instead of shelling out a less noticeable sum every now and then; and for the publisher, the money's in the bag with another reader secured for the year ahead. Subscription selling is particularly successful before Christmas with inducements like 'Give her a present every month/week/etc.' Marketing managers will offer to send recipients special greetings cards or reward existing subscribers who recommend friends when the friends also become subscribers. Loyalty from readers for particular titles is highly valued by magazine publishers and winning readers by subscription is usually generously repaid: one editor may set up a 'Readers Club' offering gifts and services, another could send out anniversary flowers and a third might even organise coach outings or theatre trips for subscribers in particular areas.

For modem-users the number of 'on-line' magazines is increasing and these represent a very special challenge for free-lances. Further discussion about contributing to these markets, the advantages and the problems of doing so are discussed later in this book.

A quick route to failure

A magazine editor pointed to a pile of unsolicited and unwanted copy on the floor by her desk – and sighed. 'Too many writers send unsolicited material and just hope it's what we want. If only they'd get in touch first . . . ' In an adjacent office an assistant was packing up rejected manuscripts. 'There were several good ideas in that lot but the angle was wrong. Obviously their writers hadn't studied what we want. It's such a waste of everyone's time.'

If you can't be bothered with market study, or don't take the trouble to do it thoroughly, it is just not worth sending copy to an editor and hoping for the best. Yes, you may have been 'lucky' once or have heard of someone else who has been. All the same I urge you to make contact with the editor or features editor of your target magazine *before* you have done more than write your piece in outline; perhaps (according to the nature of the subject) you may also have started researching or know how you will do so in due course. It is far wiser and ultimately more time-saving and productive to draft your idea for your eyes only so that you know what points the article will/might carry and how it would work out – and only then ask if an editor is interested in the project. At this early planning stage your piece will be easily malleable to accommodate the requirements of an interested editor – developing a point here or including another there, perhaps – and after some discussion you may well be given the go-ahead. This means, of course, nothing more than 'Let me see your completed copy.' Except in very rare cases, and then almost certainly only if the editor knows your work and what you are capable of delivering, you are not being offered a commission and the editor has not agreed to accept whatever you write.

Yes and No

It would be folly to suggest everyone can write for every market; in fact it is a blessing this is not the case or the competition to sell to magazines would be vastly increased. Maybe you will occasionally make an initial choice of market only to discover on closer study that it is really not for you at all. This could be valid reasoning but be careful not to let too many potential markets fall away with this not-for-me excuse or you'll be throwing good babies out with the bathwater; making such decisions is not easy.

So despite my constant encouragement to work hard (for that is what sustained success demands) don't always assume you can crack any market, however tough, with sheer dogged perseverance. I have sometimes ignored my own commonsense and arrogantly persisted with what proved to be an unsuitable approach or an unwanted theme. Perhaps it is only because I've wasted time, effort and had my pride dented that I now appreciate my own stupidity. In your excitement of discovering more markets than you ever thought existed and in your eagerness to write for as many of them as possible, keep a cool and controlled hold on what you are doing or your work will suffer rather than flourish. There is a limit to our capabilities, even to those of the best writers among us.

Despite the caution above, I can't resist passing on a handful of my current findings. These are quoted at random in no particular order and may not appeal to you as they do to me. Or perhaps . . .

- *Duo.* Japanese House, Studio 3, The Studios, Sheriff Road, West Hampstead, London NW6 2AR.
  This is a monthly bilingual magazine aimed at professional Japanese men and their families living in Britain. With the intention of promoting cultural and business relations between Japan and Europe, it is also for British employees of Japanese companies based in the UK.

- *Home Run.* 79 Black Lion Lane, London W6 9BG.
  Good practical articles and case studies are wanted by this ten-times-a-year publication for home-based workers.

- *Née.* VM Promotions Ltd, 17 Don Street, St Helier, Jersey, Channel Islands JE2 4TQ. Glossy monthly for women of the Channel Isles. An early copy included an invitation to readers to 'tell us your views' on Myra Hindley (which, all through a feature about her, was spelt 'Hindly'.)

Market guides

For writers there are several regularly published guides itemizing markets, with details about where to find them, as well as important information about what their editors want to buy.

1 *The Writers' & Artists' Yearbook*, A & C Black.

2 *Willings Press Guide*, Reed Information Services.

3 *The Media Guide* edited by Steve Peak and Paul Fisher, Fourth Estate Ltd.

4 *Freelance Market News*, Cumberland House, Lissadel Street, Salford, Greater Manchester M6 6GG.

4
Structure and style

It's not what you say that matters, but how you say it. That's the view of many editors, taking for granted that you approach your task with a professional attitude in choice of topic, research, length, suitability for the market, presentation – and all the practical aspects of submitting to a magazine. Of the many required writing 'skills', a distinctive yet sound style of writing with plain common sense is the most valuable. So how should we write? To blend effortlessly into everything else in the magazine? To give readers an uplift and cause them to take new interest in the page? To jolt them into noticing the manner of writing rather than its content? What is the best way to do it? What *is* style?

Did you spot that phrase 'with plain common sense' in the paragraph above? That is a large part of the answer: to write in the style of your chosen target magazine, to be acceptable in its pages as 'one of the family', yet to make readers sit up and take new interest in what they are reading – to adopt these tactics is nothing but common sense. As for jolting them into noticing how we write more than what we are writing about – that can be a dangerous way of writing and requires thought, care and restraint. But it can work well in certain circumstances. Always remind yourself that clear and simple prose is unbeatable and makes far better 'style' than all the highbrow wordiness so many people think gives weight to their words. Weight it might add, but weight seldom spells worth.

As style is the hallmark of any writer, here is a brief summary of what I think it means:

- writing with clarity;
- using plain rather than fancy words;
- using familiar rather than unusual words;
- making simple rather than complicated sentences;
- using sentences of varied length;
- using 'picture' nouns and 'action' verbs in the active voice;
- starting with vigour;

- writing as you talk;
- revising and rewriting.

Although your style is *you* just as your voice is uniquely yours, to be able to write in a style that is not naturally *you* marks your real progress as a writer. Somewhere along the route you will find your craft, personality, intelligence, and love of the written word will enable you to write in almost any style.

There is no answer to the question of what is good or bad style but that common sense we've been talking about dictates the wisdom of avoiding repetitive or monotonous word patterns, and the value of listening to what you write with the inner ear – and the outer one – by reading it aloud: better still get someone else to read it aloud to you. Vary the length and import of sentences, not by being jarringly flippant at a serious point just for the sake of it, but by bringing a clear matter-of-fact tone to help make plain what your more thoughtful work is saying.

Begin by considering which type of article you are planning to write. You will have determined to give it birth in your earlier market study so remind yourself of its exact purpose. Is it to instruct readers, to tell them something, to reflect on the past, to raise protest, to amuse, to appeal to deep feelings – or what? Editors want articles that do all these things and more. They want material of all types, but only, as we saw in the last chapter, what is relevant and timely to their magazines and policies.

Question the writer's purpose in every published article you read. What is its appeal? We may assume the subject matter is what the editor knows readers wanted or it wouldn't appear in the magazine, but how is it written? Is the style informal enough to make you feel at ease but sufficiently well-informed to give you no doubts about the value of what you are reading? Or perhaps the tone is commanding or distant, with a 'gap' between the writer and readers, i.e. written with the voice of unquestionable, even severe, authority. What is best for one market will not be ideal for other, of course, but how would you describe the article's style?

Also ask yourself if what you read is well-constructed? Do the words and sentences sit comfortably on the page so you read them without any hesitation or misunderstanding? Do you lose interest, find yourself looking back to check something in the paragraph you've just finished or realise you are skimming the whole piece quickly in the hope of spotting at least something worthwhile in it? Don't blame yourself if you are; it is the writer's fault and not yours. The article, should you ever see such a one in a magazine, suffers from a faulty or non-existent structure. In this chapter we shall consider these vital ingredients of a publishable article: its mood, its structure and its style. We'll begin by pinpointing some of the most commonly published types of article.

Being practical

If what you are writing is purely practical – giving information, perhaps – it must be logical, well ordered and do the job it sets out to do. Talk of 'style' is often superfluous as it virtually takes care of itself. A practical piece may give instructions or urge readers to some course of action. In such an article it is not hard to reach the readers. They are seeking what you are offering so you are halfway there when they settle down to read and follow your advice. This is where clear structure proves its worth. The essential ingredients are lucid organisation of information, sticking to the subject, establishing a logical sequence of points to make and adopting a style appropriate to the market. In short: contents, order and style.

Order is easy to arrange if you are instructing readers in how to build a wall, for instance, or ice a cake. Take the action in stages, dealing with each in turn and you can't fail. Although you may not write the words *first*, *next*, *then*, and so on, think of the sequence in such a way and you will be sure not to miss out any steps by mistake.

Facing facts

A 'thought' article is written to inform readers and perhaps, when they've read it, influence them to change their minds on some important topic or at least reconsider what might have been hidebound or previously unchallenged assumptions or beliefs.

Such writing needs a good deal of preparation. You will be wanting to include plenty of facts, quote opinions voiced by other people in the field under discussion, record earlier points of view, put events and statements in historical perspective: all this takes time and hard work to groom. Libraries may have to be visited, copious notes taken, interviews arranged and conducted. Background facts, possibly never to be included directly in the article itself, will be needed to support your argument or give credibility to whatever you are voicing for readers to consider.

The article will be strengthened with telling anecdotes, irrefutable figures and quotations from well-known people, all of which need finding, recording and sorting before you can use them for the effect you want to achieve. Make no mistake about it: factual articles are tricky, time-consuming and quick to trip you up if you don't get them right.

The section on 'structure plans' (later in this chapter) is essential reading before you begin.

Narrative articles

Narrative? Doesn't that mean telling a story – a fictional story? It does, but there is also scope for the narrative mode in writing articles. You may find the word 'feature' attached to this sort of article more than to others and some editors would refer to it as nothing else. In short, if you have a thumping good story to tell from the heart (and the market is suitable, of course) writing it in narrative form is often the best way.

A friend whose life I have watched closely for many years is one of this country's sufferers from a rare disease of the central nervous system. I'll call her Shirley although that isn't her real name. During one unbelievable week when she was in her mid-twenties, the disease hit Shirley with a devastation her family and friends found impossible to grasp. She was a bright, bubbly and athletic girl who was the leader of the tennis team in her first University year. Within days she changed almost beyond belief. She could not, and still cannot, move, talk, breathe unaided or even open her eyes. Able to do nothing at all for herself, she relies on the caring ministrations of other people and on an array of medical accoutrements for survival from one minute to the next. She can see if her eyelids are held open and, by some miracle, her hearing is unimpaired. Now in her mid-forties, she knows her condition will never improve and there is no possibility of a cure.

But modern technology has come to her aid. With a formidable battery of the appropriate equipment she can write and even talk. For a long time I have been struck by her marvellous sense of humour. Shirley, imprisoned in a life many people would think not worth living, cheers other folk up when they are downhearted and makes them laugh. Forgive me if I talk about her too much but this, as many editors agreed, was a story that must be told. And there were many aspects of it ...

What did those hideous days do to her young agile brain as they wrecked her body? How has she come to terms with her position since then? Does she seek an explanation? This aspect of the story, concentrating on her personal recollections, reactions and philosophy, interested most readers. It was published in two religious magazines and one of general interest with a penchant for uplifting copy gently reminding readers of their own health and good fortune. A sports title for students wanted a piece about how Shirley taught beginners tennis – yes, tennis – and wrote training handbooks for them. More than twenty magazines in several countries have published articles on a range of topics associated with her life. Some simply told her incredible story. Others were written to support those less severely handicapped and a few demonstrated how the practical aspects of caring for her could help other handicapped people. Shirley reads (or is read) everything her family and friends can find published about her and she doesn't automatically approve of it all. At times she can be grumpy, sad or impossible to please like the rest of us. But I and others know her so well we can spot when she is delighted with life, albeit she cannot display emotions as we can. She knows she is a very special celebrity and therefore someone to write about. But happy as she is as a subject, she refuses to write about herself. 'Self pity!' the words crackle out of her talking machine. 'You won't catch me going down that road.' What a girl, Shirley. What a story.

Nostalgia

Be careful with articles of this type. They are satisfying to write as they usually involve talking about our personal affairs. What is more pleasant than a nostalgic return to once-loved places and faces, happy childhood memories evoking the delights and contentment of long ago? In truth, what may have been pleasures for us in the past and are winsome to recall now are almost certainly boring for other people. Tedium is the unwitting cause of losing readers: what you are writing may be absorbing to you but to other people – think of having to look at other people's holiday photographs! And readers don't have to be polite if they don't like what's on the page in front of them. They simply turn over and remind themselves not to buy the magazine again. Dullness is a killer: a competition among sub-editors at *The Times* to see who could produce the least attractive headline came up with a winner of SMALL EARTHQUAKE IN CHILE. NOT MANY HURT. In journalism no news is bad news and dreariness is the end. That is not to say nostalgia doesn't have a valid position in a writer's armoury: it does. Just making sure you are writing for the readers and not for yourself will keep it in its proper place.

Specialised articles

Take any group of people interested in a special subject and write for them: such articles are what we might call 'specialised'. It doesn't matter what the subject is: politics, dancing, gardening, being parents, sport, pets, music, health – whatever the topic there will be a magazine about it and probably more than one. The way to write such material is to study the relevant published magazines and talk to people. We all love talking about our hobbies and special interests and you'll have no difficulty finding folk to answer all the questions you can ask. (See Chapter 8: Interviewing.)

Business and trade stories also fall into this category. They often crop up as by-products in other mainstream articles. For instance, in the course of my interview with a city financier about his millionaire status he mentioned his humble start in a small factory in Rochdale. In those days he kept a little brick in his empty sandwich box. He told me he didn't want the other men lifting the box, noticing it was light and discovering he couldn't afford any food during the working day. This was laughed off during the interview itself but made a fine start to a piece about the man in a professional journal for businessmen, where the editor favoured rags-to-riches stories about the currently famous.

A large number of articles don't readily fit into any identifiable 'slot'. That is the beauty – and the challenge – of writing non-fiction: there is nothing you cannot write about, the world is your raw material and you are restricted only by your own ability.

Structuring

Although devoted to my own electronic writing equipment (and like many other writers convinced I could not now write at length without it) I find there is still little to beat a large sheet of paper and a stout pen when the first jumbled whiffs of an idea come into my head. Any piece of writing lacking a basic plan is far more likely to founder in the writing than one given at least a simple outline of what it's trying to say and how it's going to do it.

Making a structure plan before you start will keep your head clear as you write the piece. It helps you to see where you're going, guides your arguments in the best order and stops you wandering too far from the point. A plan is as valuable to many writers, particularly at the beginning of their careers, as is an architectural design to a builder or a knitting pattern to a knitter.

Before we can make a plan we have to recognise (which doesn't mean overemphasise) the ingredients of all writing. We express what we mean using three groups of words: sentences, phrases and clauses. A basic understanding of how they differ from each other is not essential but may be helpful when we have to correct something that doesn't mean what we intended it to mean. A sentence contains at least one finite verb (i.e. a verb that has a subject it agrees with in person and number): *We strolled down the lane.* Phrases are groups of words which don't make sense on their own and have no finite verbs: *We cook in the kitchen.* Clauses cause the most trouble: they are sentences themselves and are used to join others into longer sentences: *When the children come* we will play in the garden *if it is fine.* The joiners are known as conjunctions. Words like *if, when, that* and *which* are commonly used conjunctions.

There is sound logic in the proposition that a sentence expresses one idea and a paragraph one aspect of the topic you are writing about. It is sensible because it works: articles built on this concept cause few problems to writer or reader. They are simple to understand and leave both with a feeling of satisfaction.

In this structuring method the opening sentence of each par introduces its special point which is expanded in the par's remaining sentences. ('Par' is journalist shorthand for paragraph and you'll find it often in these pages.) Clear paragraphing renders your article easy to follow as you deal with your points step-by-step.

Here is an explicit structure plan for a straightforward problem-solving, instructive or informative article:

```
Opening par = define the problem/task/topic
Par 2       = support with facts/figures/anecdotes etc
Par 3       = show how to solve/work at/gain from
              solution
Par 4       = substantiate with more examples/stories
Par 5       = wrap up with good results/spin-offs etc
```

To make a plan for your own article, marshal all your information and the points you want to present, be they at this stage on a single sheet of paper or in the form of random notes, jottings, cuttings and as yet unresearched headings. Collect everything where you can at least survey the whole range of what is likely to be your completed article. Now choose your opening point (with care, as outlined below) and mark it to take its place on a clean sheet of paper under the words OPENING PAR. Then make a note of its intended length.

If any one part of an article is more important than all the rest it is the opening and not just the first paragraph or even the first sentence. For top place in the influential stakes the opening few words win every time. Attract the instant attention of editors – indeed, rivet their attention – and they will read the rest of your copy in a receptive frame of mind. They know their readers' tastes (their jobs depend on such knowledge) and if you can please them at the beginning of your article you are off to a good start.

So a confident opening is crucial. It will set the tone and mood of the piece and provide immediate insight into the purpose of the article. Whether your subject is how to improve your swing in golf, the problems of population control in China, mending broken furniture or whatever it may be, the opening par must answer the primary question 'What's it about?'

However short you make it (I emphasise brevity because effective first pars pay dividends) the sentences should be positive and punchy or readers' eyes will wander in search of something more interesting. A short opening par gives the editor an instant indication of the article's value and needs less sub-editing when it is accepted.

The market you have chosen will determine how you word the first par, sometimes referred to as the 'lead', and there are countless ways of writing it. Start with an anecdote? A shocking revelation? A quote from a famous person?

Often you can't do better than state a simple fact:

American baseball star Hank Aron received more letters in one year than anyone has ever received before.

Perhaps you and your market prefer:

More than 900,000 letters fell on the mat last year.

Or:

Baseball sent wages soaring last year – for postmen.

As the leading par is so important we must be sure not to spoil it with rambling, shapeless or ill-planned paragraphs afterwards. While every good article begins with a strong opening, the order in which subsequent pars are arranged can make the difference between eventual success and failure.

When you read a professionally-written article you will leave it with several distinct impressions in your mind: they are there because the writer arranged the arguments and points in a particular order. This order lends weight to some important pars and allows others of less value space further on in the article. You, the reader, absorbed the result of clever paragraphing without even realising it existed: that is one proof of skilful structure planning. In the same way, arranging pars in relation to each other also needs key sentences inserted at the most meaningful points, drawing attention to important aspects of your theme where you wish to make them.

Do you have or can you find supporting matter to make sure readers are hooked? That will go in par 2 in the structure plan above as a promise that it will be worth reading what you have written.

Par 3 takes the argument further and here you would broaden your scope by bringing in a new line of reasoning or another slant on the topic. This in turn could be followed in par 4 by further substantiating anecdotes or facts to strengthen the points made in par 3.

You could continue the loop of pars 3 and 4 as many times as you feel is appropriate, introducing more new aspects and points-of-view to your story. But wait! A structured plan is only that and to follow it without variation may blight the whole work, turning it into a flat repetitive article written without much imagination or skill: a piece no editor will want because he knows no reader will be interested in reading it. 'Imagination and skill'? We shall have more to say about these vital ingredients later in this chapter.

Varying your method of sentence and paragraph construction not only makes the article easier to read but also presents a more pleasing layout on the page. There are many ways of bringing individuality to the writing of sentences, indeed such variety often lends to words and phrases richer meaning than we can convey in stereo-typed or over-used methods in daily use. So notwithstanding the value of making a structured plan before starting to write, it is worth remembering that even the most carefully-designed plan should not be adhered to regardless of the cost. The questions 'how many words should there be in a sentence?' and 'how long is a paragraph?' arise frequently in tutorial classes for beginners and there are no answers. I can only say, as with opening pars we've been discussing above, err on the side of brevity if in doubt.

Beware, likewise, of general overwriting. Your subject matter and the way you are tackling it will dictate your structure but if you are new to this writing business I urge you not to make the whole article too long. Six or seven sentences in a par usually suffice but it 'ordipends' (that's a word I thought existed when I was a child: I was amazed to discover it didn't and still feel it should). It is easy to get carried away when writing about a topic you find interesting, the more so if you are using a modern word-processor. Such a machine is a great beguiler, letting thoughts flow out of our heads as fast as our fingers can flash over the keyboard. A friend newly trained in typing at speed complains he was never tempted to overwrite when he had to fumble for each key. So much for progress!

Joiners

Those important words linking pars should be unforced and lead the reader into accepting the new par's point without difficulty. These so-called 'joiners' serve more than the purpose of linking one par to the previous one. *And* carries on with the purport of the previous par, *for* introduces a reason, a result, or a new development while *so* usually means and the consequence is, or was. An alternative viewpoint may be introduced by *but* and *now* should be used with caution: too often it means *at last we're getting to the point*.

Change for change's sake is bound to be a jerky and artificial intrusion but vary the methods of linking one paragraph to another and your prose will flow smoothly. Be sure each joiner is appropriate to its task: to bring a new point to the reader's attention.

In the sample structure plan above I refer to setting a length for each par. As with the plan itself, don't necessarily stick to your preset length come rain and shine. Although some length has to be set in the plan to let you consider how much a par's point is worth to the whole theme, as you write your article you may feel that, somehow, it is not balancing very well. Maybe a par should be shortened here or another lengthened a little there. That's perfectly all right; indeed it is an encouraging sign that your instinctive writing ability is taking over and giving you new confidence.

So forcing your work to abide by the structure plan you've made for it is a mistake: covering a point in a preset length and counting it done when you've written 50 words, say, is unnaturally fidgety and rigid if it doesn't feel right. Strictures show in structures!

On the other hand the requirement of the market regarding the length of the overall article means you cannot take all the time and space in the world to ramble on and round about in every sentence. Such diffuse and loose writing is certain to be unacceptable. Somewhere in the middle lies the best course: to write concisely and to the length required but with the article well-shaped and each paragraph or point receiving its proper proportion of the total wordage.

Signing off

If you have started with an anecdote, closing your piece with another, perhaps relating to the opening one, can give it a satisfying completeness. There are other ways of finishing off (remember a lingering farewell often kills otherwise acceptable copy) but however you do it, if you've given readers what your opening par indicated you would give them, you will have done a good job. No matter what your purpose was in writing the article, whether you've roused them to passion, soothed their fears and troubles, lulled them with fond memories or provided the solution to mending their leaky radiators, always aim to leave them contented.

Style

We've set up the framework, now what about the style? The skeleton needs clothing: back to market study we go.

Everything we need to know about a magazine's style is right there on the pages already published. What is known as 'house style' is dealt with later in this chapter but what we are studying here is the overall 'tone' of freelance material. What is it that distinguishes one piece of written work from another? That quality we so vaguely refer to as 'good': what does it really mean? The imagination and skill mentioned earlier are part of it.

To read an article or even a paragraph and be left with a glow of satisfaction is one of life's real pleasures. Most readers are happy to accept it and don't try to explain it. We writers must analyse it in some detail if we hope to encompass such easily-flowing writing in our own work. I do not believe it always comes naturally even to those apparently most skilled although I am sure the art improves with practice. We also help ourselves, perhaps without realising it, by constant and widespread reading. There are many ways of improving style and although their purpose is to make it look 'natural' their usage is, in fact, the very opposite. This is the art that conceals art; and the greatest concealment is the hiding of the tools we use and the artifices we resort to.

Stylistic tools

If you've read widely without being aware of what are termed 'figures of speech' you can be sure your reading matter has been well written. These are literary devices we writers employ to 'keep 'em reading'; they help us use words to make particular effects. Here are four of the most valuable:

Simile
Simile compares different objects by referring to what they have in common and is often preceded by *as* or *like*:

> *She sailed up in the air like Mary Poppins.*
> *She sailed up in the air as Mary Poppins did.*

Note the difference: *like* is followed by a noun but *as* comes before a clause (containing a verb).

Metaphor
This is writing in a figurative sense, creating a picture image:

> *He hit the nail on the head.*

It also compares two things without using *like* or *as*:

> *The plan was a dead duck.*

Note: Simile says one thing is *like* another: metaphor says one thing *is* another.

Euphemism
Softening the impact of something hard for readers to accept is achieved by euphemism – clothing it in elaborate words:

> *I regret your services are no longer required.* (You're sacked.)

Idiom
Every language has its own little quirks and oddities: this is idiom. Between themselves English speakers don't have to explain what they mean by *a fly in the ointment* or *she's the one who wears the trousers*. There are countless other idiomatic phrases that

embroider our language and writers for magazines should not be frightened of using them. Wisely handled they can add richness and variety.

Rhythm

Have you thought of written work, printed words on sheets of paper, as having pulses and cadences? These determine the overall effect on the 'inner' eye and the pleasure (or otherwise) brought to the senses. Does what you've written have rhythm, albeit in words and not music? For there is undoubtedly a pleasing word rhythm and all the best writing, whatever its *genre*, has it.

It may be a question of unison. In the article's sections (its architectural divisions, as we discuss below) is it one family? Does the introduction strike a chatty informal tone, is the middle formal or pompous? And what is the tone of the later parts or the end – neither formal nor chatty, but stilted or vague? Of course I have to exaggerate the problem to make my point plain: there should be, indeed there must be, rapport in the separate parts if the piece is to read as an harmonious whole. Lack of accord often makes readers feel uneasy: it's as if they realise something is amiss but can't quite put their fingers on what it is and a small bit of their trust and anticipation in what they are reading is lost.

An example: I love skating and chocolate. If compatibility is to be maintained the objects of the verb love should be constructed in the same way. In this case the first object of love is skating which is a noun (in technical terms a *gerund*) formed from the verb to skate. The second object of love is chocolate, another noun. Somehow the pairing of a gerund and a noun, unequal partners, brings the reader up with a jerk. You may have noticed how effective such writing can be when used deliberately, perhaps for comic effect. In these cases the whole point is, of course, that it does sound odd and therefore will give us a laugh because it is not what we expect. But be wary of using it in ignorance. Stage pianists know you have to be able to play the piano well before you can play it *badly* well.

It is easy to correct errors in harmony and there are countless ways of skinning a cat, as my grandmother used to say; as a devoted ailurophile (off to the dictionary for you?) the sentence still makes me shudder.

Clarity

I have an obsession with clarity. But I do not apologise. If you, the reader of this book, gain nothing else from it but the conviction that clarity is the over-riding quality essential to all good writing, you will have learned the most valuable fact any writer can learn. If you can't write (or learn to write) so readers can understand what you've written you will never succeed. Perhaps your structure is weak or your research has been inadequate. Do either 'show through'? That's a bad error and one difficult for us writers to spot, seeing it all subjectively. Maybe you've been talking in the wrong language, using words and phrases unsuitable for the readership. Misunderstanding has many causes. And it all adds up to lack of clarity.

I like the story of a public house in the West Midlands called 'The Bird-in-Hand'. The landlord faced complaints about its new sign showing a curvaceous bikini-clad blonde. He explained he had simply asked the signwriter for a bird.

Tautology

The shortest way of saying what you want to say is often the best. Many words we use in speech are redundant, not necessary and would be better omitted. Those last few can go for a start. *Not necessary* and *would be better omitted* mean the same as redundant.

Phrases like *advanced towards* and *reconsider again* don't need their hangers-on: advancing can only mean going towards and anyone reconsidering anything is already considering it again. In formal speech tautology is evidence of poor construction (or perhaps a nervous delivery) and in casual conversation it is generally harmless for it has gone before we think it worth noting. In the written word it is inexcusable.

Accuracy

Not only must facts be accurate: words must be well-chosen for their purpose. To each of us a particular word or group of words represents an image in our minds and we are only able to communicate with each other because, by and large, we share the same words for the same images. Communication depends on mutual understanding just as safe motoring depends (among other things) on drivers knowing what traffic lights mean and what road signs are telling us. But when we listen to someone talking in a language we don't understand no 'image-transfer' takes place: we don't know the words used or what images they are trying to send us.

So all effort spent on fine phraseology, thoughtful structuring, earth-shattering revelations and the many aspects of article writing that take up our time are totally wasted if we do not use the 'right' words for the job. Only they will transfer the image you want passed from your head into that of your readers: the wrong words will move only part of the image or none of it. Worse still, they will create in your readers a concept quite different from the one you think you are giving them.

What if you need to use a particular word or a term but cannot be sure your readers will understand its meaning? Tact is called for; you don't want to exasperate them by over-explanation or annoy them by treating them as if they were half-witted. If you don't use the word or term in a context that itself makes the meaning clear, give a very short explanation in brackets directly after using it. Brevity and immediacy should avoid rousing readers' ire as they assume the explanation is for others less intelligent.

Following fashion . . .

Clarity undoubtedly begins at home. (Here I can't resist voicing my long-held dissatisfaction about the language of scoring in cricket. In this sport, whose jargon must bemuse any student of English, 'Smith bowled Jones' doesn't mean 'Smith bowled Jones out of the game.' Oh, no. 'Smith bowled Jones' actually means 'Smith was bowled out by Jones.' Illogically, on the cricket pitch, the active voice becomes passive and *vice versa*. So 'Smith bowled Jones' means 'Jones bowled Smith.' Wherever clarity begins, it does not even *exist* in cricket.)

Language is constantly changing and is rich in words of every colour and degree and somewhere, if the writer can find it, is the word, the *only* word, for each occasion. Where better to look than in a dictionary?

With a history stretching back more than 150 years, *The Chambers Dictionary* is unrivalled in its coverage and character. Can a dictionary have character? Certainly – when its wide-ranging entries reflect the richness and diversity of English from Shakespeare's time to the present day. The sciences, commerce, politics, the media, the arts, slang, the environment – these are just some of its unsurpassed coverage in every field of human endeavour. Explanations are clear and waffle-free, words are easy to find and definitions simple to understand. There are useful appendices, too, of foreign words, the Bible, weights and measures, and Latin and Greek alphabets. With over 2000 pages, this largest single volume English dictionary will strengthen your vocabulary and writing-power every time you open its pages. More than a writer's tool, it is every wordsmith's delight. £25.00 hardback.

The most famous English dictionary in the world (as well as being the most comprehensive) is now also available on a compact disk. This is *The Chambers Dictionary on CD-ROM* and it is available for PC Windows and Macintosh computer users. With well over half a million references and definitions, this computer dictionary is an ideal factual source. It is up-to-date and authoritative and enables thematic searches for a particular word or phrase, the use of 'wild cards' when only part of a definition is known and easy print out of all or any part of an entry. There is also unrivalled coverage of new, technical and literary words. You want the complete, instant and faultless solution to spelling and definition problems? If you run a CD-ROM drive with your computer – here it is. £45.00 including VAT.

Ah, you may be thinking, but what merit is there in the writer finding just the 'right' word if the reader cannot understand it? Now we're back with our old friend: in this writing business most roads lead to market study, and here – again – we find the answer to how much we should or dare venture outside the market's published vocabulary. Once more common sense is the best guide.

All writers love words and I would like to try a few unusual ones in copy for popular and consumer magazines that don't normally use them. Eleemosynary – now there's a gorgeous word. Shall I use it? And what about omnivorous, camaraderie, vulpine and aficionado? Dare I try them? I know that for the type of markets mentioned above the answer is 'No' for I do not court rejection. So I must confine my passion for readers of this book who share with me the endless bliss to be found in a dictionary. A speaker on radio describes his burden as ineluctable, scholars seek recondite explanations and a Cumbrian farmer is philo-sophical about spending his life in ordure. I warm to them all for the words they choose. It's not that we writers have to be mere followers of others in selecting the words we use; many so-called 'new' words and phrases were originally coined by journalists. But while untried ideas frequently command editorial approval, 'new' words are more likely to earn rejection and never be tested on magazine readers.

Occasionally we discover a word that seems to have moved the 'wrong' way in its development and here I am thinking of one virtually unacceptable on the printed page. It doesn't deserve its present poor reputation as its past was an attempt to avoid giving the very offence it now causes. In seventeenth century London Old Bailey clerks used many home-made acronyms; one concerned prostitutes who were recorded as having been taken into custody For Use of Carnal Knowledge.

If the unfamiliar words a couple of paragraphs above sent you scurrying to a dictionary can we rely on casual readers doing the same? Alas we cannot. Many magazines are sold on nothing more than the browse-like-buy impulse. Far from encouraging readers, such etymological indulgence (see how difficult it is to stop once you start?) will drive them away at the gallop. We must forget our personal likes and dislikes, come down to earth and look at what the reader wants and will buy.

I have generally found it wise to stick pretty closely to the language markets expect in my initial dealings with them, growing cautiously more venturesome as my reliability becomes established. Sometimes I've come unstuck at this point (growing too big-headed) and what I thought was a good market for me has decided I am not the writer it wanted after all. There could be many reasons for losing what I had hoped was a steady buyer of my copy: one of them might be that I'd strayed into using my choice of words in preference to theirs.

Before we leave the theme of words, a warning: be careful of trade names. So many have almost merged into daily language we hardly recognise them as such but using them in a magazine article could cause problems. Hoovering the carpet, Sellotaping things together and playing with Lego may seem harmless occupations until advertisers of non-Hoover vacuum cleaners, non-Sellotape adhesives and non-Lego toys protest at the free plugs given to their rivals. No magazine can afford to invite such trouble and wise writers do not provide copy likely to start law suits.

Clichés

Clichés fall into the same potential pit: chiefly because of the old argument about their viability in 'good' writing. Moth-eaten ones are not hard to spot but often a phrase that seemed particularly appropriate at the time someone first used it (which is seldom the time we first noticed it) gains rapid popularity. Then brilliance dulls into tedium and the big family of hackneyed clichés welcomes another member. Should you avoid such words or groups of words? In determination to do so you can fall over backwards (an old one) and risk the studious avoidance of them showing through your work. If you suspect your vocabulary is not yet adequate to transforming the original brilliance of a cliché into your own words an artificial avoidance of it may involve a tortuous trip round the houses (sic), leaving the very point you wish to make floundering without a supporting framework. Perhaps you never think in terms of clichés anyway, let alone other people's. Lucky you.

A schoolboy's answer

'Syntax,' repeated the schoolboy, giving himself time to think of an answer to the question. 'Syntax is putting words in order so they mean the same as the order you've put them in.'

He had the right basic idea. Syntax is the grammatical structure of individual sentences: the correlation of one word to another, one phrase to another and one clause to another. It is by no means as fearsome as it sounds and most of us speak and write all our lives using correct syntax without even being conscious of it.

It is only when it breaks down that we realise how important it is and how much we need to understand its function. An offer from a local television shop came with this invitation:

As an existing customer we have a superb offer for you.

That doesn't make sense because I am the customer, not the shop. Sometimes a sentence says quite the opposite of what you mean it to say. I saw the following published in a leading pet magazine as part of a reader's letter:

After suffering bladder trouble for some time the vet has recommended our dog has an operation.

I don't think we are expected to commiserate with the vet but that is exactly what the letter suggests. 'So what?' you may argue. 'We know it means the dog has been suffering, not the vet, so what is wrong with the sentence?' Of course we know what it means but that is not what it *says*. Dial 999 for syntax!

Since it's a matter of putting the words in the right order in relation to each other a simple dissection of the delinquent sentence will cure its ills, if not the dog. Copy its two halves out separately and consider where they should be to earn their keep. This is just one way to rearrange them (there are others equally effective) so there's no doubt about who was suffering and no hilarity raised by an unintentional howler:

> *When our dog had suffered bladder trouble for some time the vet recommended an operation.*

Often putting the clauses and phrases in the wrong order causes confusion. Imagine you wrote:

> *Burglars broke into my house which was damaged by fire when I was away on holiday.*

This could be understood as:
   1) the fire occurred when the burglars broke in.
or 2) the fire occurred when I was away on holiday and burglars broke in on a later occasion.

The original sentence makes three statements:
   [burglars broke into my house]
   [which was badly damaged by fire]
   [when I was away on holiday]

Change it to one of these to make your meaning clear:

1 Burglars who broke into my house when I was on holiday set it on fire.

2 My house was damaged by fire when I was away on holiday and then burglars broke into it.

Words, words, words

George Abbott, the famous Broadway producer who lived to be 107, was a stickler for correct word usage. At a mere 98 he was escorting the new wife he had married only a year earlier when he tripped and fell. His bride was distraught.

'Get up, George!' she cried, bending over him, 'Don't just lay there!'

He shuddered and looked at her sternly. 'Lie,' he said.

A newsreader spoke on radio of one warring faction 'decimating' another. 'At least 80 of the force of 200 were killed,' he stated. Had they been decimated, just 20 would have been lost, for 'decimate' means kill one in ten. So let us try to be accurate in our choice of words.

If you're totally baffled by the meaning of a word you could follow the example of a teacher conducting a class in the study of *The Merchant of Venice*. When he drew their attention to *'The quality of mercy is not strain'd,'* a boy raised his hand to ask a question. 'Please sir, is that strained as in straining a rope or strained meaning put through a sieve?' There was a silence while the teacher realised he didn't know the answer. Then a mixture of inspiration and logic came to his rescue. 'As it was not strained,' he emphasised, 'the question is irrelevant.'

Too many of us have memories of grammar we'd rather not recall: schooldays darkened by teachers trying to implant what seemed inflexible and pointless rules into our heads. Adverbs do this, prepositions must not do that, transitive verbs behave differently from intransitive ones, something agrees with or governs something else – oh, who wants or needs to bother with grammar? Why don't we forget it and get on with writing?

Take heart. Grammar is an essential part of language not an immutable set of rules to be followed slavishly. Language is changing all the time despite dyed-in-the-wool purists who deplore the use of 'modern' words, and so it must. If it hadn't developed over the centuries we should still be talking in Anglo-Saxon or whatever tongue was in use when a nothing-must-change law began.

No matter how good your command of grammar, spelling and the use of special stylistic techniques, if you do not construct an article on a solid grammatical foundation you will not make a success of it. It's such an important job there are even computer software programs providing templates to make it easier. Such is the proliferation of these aids I leave you to select one that will help your work and sit comfortably in your computer. Before anyone throws this book down in horror let me mollify purists by confessing I eyed such programs with initial doubts. Now, having investigated several thoroughly, I realise my hesitation was born of ignorance. Everyone, even the most articulate writer, can make foolish errors. In one quick pass a well-constructed computer program can locate mistakes in grammar, punctuation and readability. In no way can it teach someone how to write but I am confident it will be a real help to those who need it. At dubious points in your text most programs pause and suggest how they may be corrected, giving you the option of ignoring any such suggestions, making alterations or rewriting your copy in your own way; at every pause for possible correction you can ask for – and receive – an explanation of the relevant grammatical rule.

Other computer programs proofread your writing for mistakes in style as well as grammar. Because some types of writing require the writer to pay closer attention to grammar and style than others these programs are designed to guide you in many predefined styles as well as to help you customise your own. Is your current work technical, general, advertising, a report, journalistic, documentation – or what? In any of these styles a sophisticated program also differentiates between standard, formal and informal – so the choice is wide.

Punctuate or be damned

How's the punctuation in your life? Are your full stops happy and do commas put their feet up on your hearth? And what about exclamation marks? Is direct speech a danger area? In short, does your punctuation need a face-lift? It shouldn't be a problem if you remember its twin purposes are:

1 to make your writing smooth and easy to read;

2 to ensure what you have written is not misunderstood.

Like other subdivisions of grammar, faulty punctuation raises a wall between the writer and readers by making them pause and reconsider, frown, maybe try again – and probably turn to a new page of the magazine. The rules of grammar and punctuation were not carved in stone with wicked glee by scholars anxious to trip you up. They exist to ease communication and for no other reason. If you remain sceptical and fear I am going to lumber you with yet another set of instructions amended from those you might have battled with years ago, delight in an acknowledgment that sometimes grammar isn't all it's cracked up to be and has to admit defeat. For example, the current lack of a both-sexes pronoun is a major shortcoming ...

He, she or it

Traditionalists often decry the introduction of 'new' words to our language so I doubt they would support my idea of introducing a multi-gender pronoun. What a relief it would be if we could put an end to the wearisome business of she/he, his/her etc. As no such unisex pronoun exists, apart from 'one', a usage now outdated in common parlance and used only in deliberately formal or official mode, what is the best way round the problem?

Turning the singular into the plural often makes no difference to the context or sense of a sentence: let *a shopkeeper should always lock and bar his or her shop* become *shopkeepers should always lock and bar their shops*.

Superfluous words may be deleted: *the infant will need treatment if he or she is to recover* may become *the infant will need treatment to recover*.

A single word may replace a phrase: *the applicant wrote it by himself or herself* evades the gender problem as *the applicant wrote it unaided*.

On the house

If you hope to sell to a magazine you can improve your chances of acceptance by observing and following what is known as the 'house style.' This is merely an accepted pattern of uniformity adhered to for the sake of tidiness and clarity. How, for instance, do you write numbers and figures? Should it be 'Three blind mice' or '3 blind mice'? 'A boy of 6' or 'A boy of six'? Which is better – 'There are 31 days in May' or 'There are thirty-one days in May'?

Taking note of the house style of your intended market is part of market study itself. That means you will get to know a great deal about how the editor likes the magazine to look. You will know the favoured habits in punctuation, paragraphing, the use of capital letters and hyphens, writing numbers, dates, abbreviations and everything else that will appear as text on the magazine pages.

Adhering to an established house style means, for example, that there is no uncertainty about whether to write 'Doctor Brown' or 'Dr. Brown' – with or without the point.

Keeping to the house style is not just a matter of placating an editor; inconsistencies not only irritate typesetters but also cause confusion. The purpose of house style is to ensure there is none. Time was when house style books were tossed around in magazine and newspaper offices. Nowadays with word-processors on every desk the old books seem to have vanished. But don't imagine house style doesn't matter any more just because nobody can produce a style book. I know of magazine offices where the word-processors in the features department have several aspects of house style built in. So staff writers cannot write Dec 25th 1999, for instance, when they should be writing 25 December 1999. That's how important house style is!

If you fail to observe the required house style a sub-editor may change your copy so it follows the rules in every respect. Although you may find this irksome, be thankful your solecisms were not enough for your work to be rejected – and determine to do better with your next submission.

Sub-editors have their individual preferences but are obliged to follow the house style of the magazine or group employing them. Their job is to make all copy conform to the house style in voice, spelling, English and punctuation. They check that facts and arguments are logically presented (although work seldom requires major surgery as it would not have been accepted in the first place) and scrutinise copy for libel. It is an absorbing job but exposure to it can lead to an involuntary mental 'subbing', as it is called, of everything you see or read!

Your chosen market's house style will be your best guide but there are a few general rules to observe in the absence of any others:

Avoid 'alot', 'diningroom' and other falsely merged words: ' a lot' and 'dining room' are correct. And watch out for too liberal a sprinkling of hyphens. (But don't go to the other extreme as headline writers sometimes do. In a local newspaper in Avon I saw report headed MOTHER TO BE KILLED. Beside it was an announcement reading PICTURES – PRINCESS ANNE IN BATH.)

Spell out whole numbers up to twenty (four, seven, eighteen and so on) but use Arabic numerals for 21 and higher. It would be foolish, for example, to write 'the bill came to nineteen thousand four hundred and sixty seven pounds and eighty three pence.' Start sentences with 'Seven days make a week' rather than '7 days make a week' but in identifying a year '1993 began on a Friday' is always preferred to 'Nineteen-ninety-three ...' Be careful about decades and spare the apostrophes: 'the 1920s were wild' is correct: the '1920's were wild' is not.

Talking of apostrophes, you know a lady lives in a lady's house but are you sure lots of ladies live together in a ladies' house? To remind you; the apostrophe is placed after either the single or plural form of a noun in the possessive case. The most frequent apostrophic (I don't know whether there is such a word or whether I have just invented it) intruder is that in 'it's'. In an Arts Council brochure, no less, I read 'This successful community storytelling project is now into it's third year.' The guilty apostrophe is so frequently inserted or omitted in error there is a danger of its misuse being ignored and accepted on the grounds that the correct usage is too much trouble to observe and it doesn't matter anyway. Over my dead body!

Henry VIII and other monarchs command Roman figures as do Popes, other ordinal dignitaries and some American offspring of tradition-building parents (Arnold Zimmer II) with the 'I' typed as a capital 'I' and not the number 1 or lower case 'l'.

Study the pages of your chosen title for dates: May 8, May 8th, 8 May or 8th May? What about months? Nov or November, Feb or February etc? And years: do they come before the month, before the day but after the month – or how? How does the magazine deal with fractions – half, 1/2 or .5? And what about 'per cent' or '%'? Taking the trouble to note these and other small points of usage and making your own copy observe the same rules will give the editor an instantly favourable impression that you have bothered to study the magazine. It will also endear you to the sub-editors who will be spared the chore of having to amend the presentation of figures and numbers inconsistent with their house style.

Be your own sub-editor

Before submitting your copy to an editor (or even presenting it to yourself in its final print-out) go through it with an eagle's eye. The ability to edit your own work is in many a professional journalist's opinion the secret of quality writing. It involves stepping outside your baby and viewing it dispassionately as if you were seeing it for the first time. If that weren't difficult enough you then have to whip it into shape with a degree of cold purposefulness tantamount to self-flagellation. Excess wordage must be whittled away and some of your cherished phrases pulverised in your determination to prune and sharpen the article to its ideal balance within its word length. It is a hard and painful task but it must be done. Perhaps if we remember we are partly doing it instinctively all the time it won't hurt so much. And it is a comfort to know the more writing we do the easier it becomes.

You could begin by making sure you are specific in what your article is saying. 'I've been to several countries in Europe but had never seen this . . . ' is more meaningful when you change it to 'France, Spain, Germany, Holland – but this was new to me . . . ' Scrutinise your adjectives, a common cause of flat predictable sentences, as it is easy to drift into the habit of assuming every noun needs a descriptive Siamese-twin. An adjective should only earn a place on your page when it has something worthwhile to say, to add a meaning or an extra dimension that is valid at that point and cannot be said better in any other way. Spot the baddies, cut or replace them and their cousins, adjectival phrases, and then do the same with adverbs and their associated phrases, tidying up as you go. Sorry, all you *verys* and *reallys* and similar woolly-word trespassers – out! And thinking of *verys* it pays to be cautious about superlatives. Write that your neighbour's cat has the longest whiskers of any in England and you're asking for trouble. Somebody somewhere may produce a cat sporting longer whiskers. What is worse, your editor might no longer feel you are the cat's whiskers about other facts and figures you give him: if you were wrong once ...

Delete anything not essential. I know that might mean abandoning some privately-popular sentences and paragraphs but are they there only or mainly because they appeal to you? Excessive self-indulgence may be contrary to the rules of pleasing the reader. If in doubt about the relevance of a particular piece picture yourself in the shoes of a typical reader. And remember an old maxim: if in doubt, cut it out.

Are you constantly editing your work? Perhaps you do it as you write it or in slabs at the end of a day's work or when you've completed the whole piece. Whatever your method, never feel you are frittering away your time. Rewriting (which is what editing your own work amounts to) is never dissipated effort and few of us do enough. For beginners it is particularly difficult; even acknowledging that it must be done is hard. But doing it frequently means the difference between rejection and acceptance.

5
Research

When you are bursting with ideas and eager to turn them into saleable articles you know you will need a great deal of information – accurate and as up-to-date as you can find – to support your project. Just where do you find it? There are countless research sources, not all of them are in book form, and it is a comfort to know that somewhere, someone has the exact information you want.

Research is more than checking the truth (or otherwise) of bald facts, a good deal more. It means you must make yourself an expert, if only for the time of writing, on your chosen topic. Your research must give you the confidence and authority to write positively. Listen to experts talking about their special subjects: you accept that they know far more than they reveal and because you understand this, you can accept their views and opinions without hesitation.

Don't let the mere thought of research deter you. Make a start, however tentative, and you will discover how engrossing it is. It's as if delving into facts about the topic you already find fascinating increases your enthusiasm – and you will soon find yourself inspired with new ideas as your research progresses. I know several writers who become so addicted to research it's hard for them to call a halt and get down to writing.

For each new job, i.e. one involving a topic you have not worked on previously, you have to decide what facts will be needed and what may be useful information to hold on the side, perhaps for use at a later date when writing on the same topic for another market. While finding both these you must also avoid getting side-tracked. I know that I can't think ahead about a project unless I keep careful records of all research (detailing where I found information and when) and this system proves invaluable if anyone ever queries my copy either before or after publication. Imagine having to do mountains of research all over again just to discover where you found the answer the first time!

Making a start

- What do you need to know?
- What else would it be useful to know, even if you only use it as background knowledge for the current project?
- What would it be wise to mark as 'for future development and expansion'?

I generally start with three files for assembling information in the above categories. With every fact or piece of useful information in all three files, I keep my own notes or observations – which are decidedly scrappy at an early stage. As the three files grow it is usually the 'for future development' one that gets the thickest. Didn't I promise research is an inspiration for more ideas? Also in the files go newspaper or magazine cuttings, bits and bobs, promisingly useful or helpful titbits I come across anywhere (and I never stop looking). I have a personal method of data security you might like to follow; when filing a scrap of information I haven't yet had time to check I mark it with a big red question mark on the back. A big red question mark means CHECK IT!

Reference sources

So where do you look? As your needs will not be identical to mine or anyone else's when it comes to the specialist topics you are writing about, I will list some of the books that benefit us all, regardless of what we write. Topping the list is every writer's treasure-chest on how to set about research:

Research for Writers by Ann Hoffmann, A & C Black, 35 Bedford Row, London WC1R 4JH. £11.99.

An invaluable handbook firmly established as an indispensable research guide offering a wealth of sound advice and solid data for every serious writer. The latest edition has been fully revised and expanded and now provides up-to-date information and new reference works, recent developments in information science and the many sources open to writers. It also covers the procedures for tracing out-of-print books and obtaining books and information from and about countries overseas. Contents include factual and historical research, organisation and method, where to find what you are looking for, family and local history, genealogy, picture research, and much more . . .

Whitaker's Almanack, J Whitaker & Sons, 12 Dyott Street, London
WC1A 1DF. £30.00.

The world in a volume, this is a unique guide to British and
world affairs. Whatever you are writing, in these 1247 pages
you will find thousands of invaluable facts to help you.
Whitaker's is extensively revised each year to ensure that every
section is comprehensive and claims to hold more information
on the UK and the rest of the world than any other single-
volume reference book. But beware! Browsing becomes addictive and you may find this book hard to put down.

The Media Guide edited by Steve Peak and Paul Fisher, Fourth
Estate Ltd, 6 Salem Road, London W2 4BU. £12.00.

Contacts, to a journalist, are everything and being able to build
up a reliable list is an enormous help in researching for any
project. For just as knowing how to find facts is more valuable
than knowing facts, so knowing whom to ask is the most valuable of all. 'I don't know, but I know a man/woman who does,'
is more than just a comic catch phrase. 'Outside' contacts are
generally quite easy to establish but it is not always possible to
find them packed so handily into a single small paperback.
Here are key telephone numbers to the Houses of Parliament,
courts, local government bodies, police and ambulance stations,
pressure groups, quangos, embassies, Departments of State, the
European Commission, trade unions, national sports centres,
ombudsmen, coastguards and countless more important links.
Perhaps a journalist's most precious contacts are those established over years of work in touch with other people. As a start
to such a list this book provides useful information on cross-
media ownership, the Internet, think tanks, lobbyists, marketing
magazines and year books. Lists of top-selling magazines and
their publishers, picture agencies and libraries, as well as telephone numbers of almost all consumer magazines makes this
an information-packed manual no serious writer can afford to
lack.

The Cambridge Factfinder edited by David Crystal, Cambridge
University Press. £9.95.

What is a fact? It's not an easy question to answer for a fact is
seldom a single isolated item of information. An inquiring
writer may be seeking confirmation of a single fact but a first-

class factbook will offer extensions to the original query by putting it into perspective. You asked about X and here's the answer but don't forget there's also Y and Z which can help you understand X further. So take a look at Y and Z as well. This is the guiding principle of *The Cambridge Factfinder* whose 715 pages are crammed with over 180,000 facts. You want to know when traffic lights were invented, who played the drums in Bill Haley and his Comets, or how many people in the world speak Italian as their native tongue? Which countries joined the United Nations in 1990? What is the area of the Isle of Wight? How long do starlings live? Unique among reference books, this is a vast archive of information and a wonderful solution to the sort of questions that cannot be addressed to a conventional encyclopaedia. Easy to consult (even the comprehensive index runs to more than 125 pages) here is a book that must surely have a place on every writer's shelf.

Bamber Gascoigne Encyclopedia of Britain, Macmillan. £29.95.

'The Cutty Sark was a three-masted tea-clipper designed to carry tea from India to the London market.' Correct? No. 'The BBC programme *Tomorrow's World* was first transmitted in 1962.' Wrong. 'An International Music Eisteddfod is held each year at Llandudno.' Wrong again.[1] It is so easy to make small mistakes. But in print, especially tens of thousands or hundreds of thousands of times (as in the case of popular high-circulation magazines) what began as a split second's error or just a press of the wrong key on a keyboard is bound to annoy innumerable readers. You may only realise you've made a mistake when protests arrive and by that time there will be little or nothing you can do to make amends. Editors dislike printing apologies in subsequent editions but they will certainly take note of writers who cause them trouble and give the magazine a bad name if the level of protest is high. So it pays to check and double-check your facts. As for the mistakes above, you won't make them if you have at your fingertips this impressive volume described by publisher Macmillan as 'the A-Z of Britain's past and present.' The author casts his net wide to cover a feast of facts and statistics about British history, politicians, pop musicians, sports personalities, businesses, literature, architecture, art, scandals, disasters, battles and current affairs. Described by the Library

[1] In case lack of the right answers keeps you awake at night, they are, respectively, 'from China' 'in 1957' and 'at Llangollen.'

Review as 'a highly successful attempt to distil virtually a reference library into a single work', this is a book about everything.

The Guinness Dictionary of Quotations For All Occasions, compiled
by Gareth Sharp. £6.99.

'Reading is to the mind what exercise is to the body.' So said Irish
dramatist Richard Steele who founded the *Tatler* in 1709 and the
Spectator two years later. That will be a comfort to bookworms,
especially if they have a passion for quotations. Writing about
what other people have said, rejoicing in the reflections of the
famous, the wisdom of the experienced and the *mots justes* of the
witty – these are pleasures freely enjoyed by us all and there are
many publications designed to help us do it. 'When a thing has
been said and said well, have no scruple. Take it and copy it.'
Those words introduce the *Guinness Dictionary of Quotations For
All Occasions* (where the author of the above is revealed) which is
a paperback packed with gems drawn from a wide variety of
sources. It is sensibly arranged (no more of that fruitless search
for the 'right' quotation) with the contents embracing the light-
hearted, the more profound and a great deal in between.
Misquoting is a quick path to trouble and just one mistake can
involve you in irksome and unwelcome correspondence.

The following societies and organisations may also prove
helpful:

1 British Guild of Travel Writers, 90 Corringway, London W5
3HA. Provides help for professional travel writers.

2 Fellowship of Christian Writers, 9 Windsor Road, Kingsbridge,
Devon TQ7 1BX.
Members include beginners, part-time and full-time writers.

3 Medical Journalists' Association, 185 High Street, Stony
Stratford, Milton Keynes MK11 1AP.
Provides a forum for mutual discussion of interests common to
medical writers.

4 Society of Authors, 84 Drayton Gardens, London SW10 9SB.
Promotes and protects the interests of authors and writers.

5 The Outdoor Writers' Guild, 27 Camwood, Clayton Green,
Bamber Bridge, Preston, Lancs PR5 8LA.

Libraries

A local library is the first port of call for most writers. There you may consult (with the help of the staff perhaps) library catalogues on microfiche which exist for you to use as well as for the librarian. Easy instructions generally accompany an on-line or CD-ROM catalogue and even if you have never touched a computer keyboard before you will not find it hard to operate.

Subject indexes lead you to classification numbers for the information you need and may also guide you along allied routes you'll find helpful. Librarians are trained and experienced in replying to your questions and you can save them and yourself time by being prepared. Be as precise as possible and explain why you want to know something if it helps in the search for it; a good librarian may suggest avenues of research that have not occurred to you.

A brief awareness of how the Dewey Decimal Classification works will help you find your way about on the library shelves. This is the system all British Public libraries use to file their books. It divides information into 10 sectors, (hence the use of the word decimal) each with its own subdivisions, thus:

000 General works
100 Philosophy
200 Religion
300 Social sciences
400 Languages
500 Science
600 Technology
700 Arts and recreation
800 Literature
900 Geography, biography and history

In pubic libraries you will also find trade directories with thousand of entries.

Most standard reference books may only be consulted on library premises and may not be taken away, and of course not every library can stock every book you want to consult but help is at hand in the shape of the Inter-Library Loan Scheme which enables branch libraries to obtain virtually any book. You may have to pay a small charge. The rarer the book you want, or the more distant its eventual location, the longer you could wait for it to be delivered to your local library.

If you don't know or are not sure of the title of the book you are looking for a general survey of your topic can be invaluable. To my own surprise, I often find looking at children's books will help clarify a complex subject I want to learn about and which – initially – is something of a foggy muddle in my mind. The Civil War, for example, was simply explained and gave me the first clear reminder of what I'd forgotten (or never knew) from my schooldays. So be ready to read children's books first.

Then ask your librarian if the library stocks the *Aslib Directory of Information Sources in the UK*. This reliable guide tables almost 7,000 sources of information, listing organisations which charge for supplying it as well as those ready to issue it for nothing. The directory will reveal names and addresses of libraries holding their own information; from here it is a matter of contacting the secretary or named person to confirm when, where and how their records may be consulted.

Many larger libraries, especially in major towns and cities, also stock back numbers of magazines and will let you borrow them for market study.

Photocopying

Facilities or making photocopies are available in virtually all reference libraries and record offices and it is possible to make your own copies of material that is out of copyright. So frequent is the unauthorised use of photocopiers that many people forget the law of the land, which is this: unless you have written permission from the copyright-owner to copy what you want without restriction, you are allowed to copy just one item at a time from a newspaper or magazine or book. Officially you may be asked to sign a statement that your photocopying is for private purposes only, although in practice many librarians are too busy (or too casual?) to enforce this obligation.

Even less fussy about whether you are breaking the law or not are the 'copy shops' to be found in every High Street. All they are bothered about is that you pay the cost of operating their machines – so moral scruples about what infringement of copyright may mean to its holder rests on your shoulders. Just remember one day someone else may be 'stealing' your work in this way and ask yourself whether you will think such action is fair practice.

When you feel your local public libraries cannot offer the information you require you will need to spread your search further afield. Access is free to the general public at larger city and regional reference libraries. The British Library, despite many troubles in relocation to its new home at 96 Euston Road (between Euston and King's Cross stations), has a tradition of housing a huge range of information to be found in no other library but you don't go in and browse around as you might do in your local library. Firstly you have to obtain a Reader's ticket – and these are not freely allocated. You must produce worthy and valid reasons for your application. Even when you are granted a ticket you identify what you want only by consulting catalogues. Once you've located it you fill in a form asking for your choice but you may have a lengthy wait before it is in your hands. Sometimes the whole day passes, your ticket expires and the book has still not arrived.

Reference and copyright libraries

One (free) copy of every book published in the UK is deposited in the British Library, the Bodleian Library in Oxford, Cambridge University Library, the National Library of Wales in Aberystwyth, the National Library of Scotland in Edinburgh and Trinity College in Dublin. University and museum libraries are comprehensive but not always easy to gain access to without written evidence of your credibility and in some cases recommendation is expected from an authoritative person such as a University professor or the Head of a Department.

Most British officials and government publications, except those recently issued or published, may be found in the larger reference libraries and at the Public Records office at Ruskin Avenue, Kew, Richmond, Surrey TW9 4DU (tel: 0181 876 3444) which holds records covering the last eight hundred years. The Guildhall Library specialises in records relevant to the City of London from the same period. Remember, too, that Government departments have press officers issuing press releases which are often very useful and informative. Consult public relations' officers (PROs) for information and, wherever you go, always ask for press packs or PR handouts. Contacts from government, business, industry, education, trade, institutions and leisure organisations welcome good publicity and are glad to help with queries. For instance, The European Parliament UK Office (2 Queen Anne's Gate, London SW1H 9AA. Tel: 0171 222 0411) is where to discover all you want to know about the European Community and its 350 million population. There are also European

Information Centres in 24 British towns and cities and a number of universities maintain European Documentation Centres. Leading magazines and newspapers have their own libraries and may be amenable to writers making genuine enquiries, particularly if prior written requests have been made.

If your story involves people or events overseas, don't omit appropriate embassies or consulates in your enquiries. In most cases the press or information office is the place to start your search. I have always found queries to such places courteously received and have often been impressed at the time and trouble my contacts will exert on my behalf, frequently offering (or even insisting) on sending back to their home countries for further information. Again, be sure to make an exact query, carefully detailing precisely what you want to find out, for a well-prepared inquiry will always elicit the best response. It may be that your chosen embassy has a library of its own to which you may be granted access. Many countries also have tourist offices in the UK with brochures and pictures to give you. (You will find more information about picture libraries in Chapter 10: Pix.) Leading companies and conglomerates such as BP and big public utilities like British Gas and ICI have worldwide interests and their press officers' job is to keep you informed, so never hesitate to ask.

It can be surprisingly difficult to research the ancestry of known families wherever they may have lived. In England parish registers began in 1538 but in many places it is impossible to trace them back to that date – or even to that century. Ministers of religion were often lax about keeping records of baptisms, marriages and funerals; record-keeping may have been spasmodic and record books may have been destroyed or just lost. A query to the local records office which should house the records you wish to search will reveal whether they exist or not. If they do, you must make an appointment to view them and expect to pay a (small) fee for doing so.

Careful copying

It's easy to drop a nought or two from the end of large numbers, easy and calamitous. So be precise when you copy them from reference books and count those noughts as carefully as any millionaire must. Likewise be scrupulous with the names, addresses, telephone numbers and the marital status of anyone you will be contacting for further reference or writing about. I mention this because people are understandably fussy about their own personal details. And when your article appears carrying the correct names and titles of high and low there will be no mistakes and you won't have upset anybody.

That's life

There can be few experiences more galling for writers than seeing their published work bearing mistakes due to careless cutting or sub-editing or – worst of all – that it misrepresents what they wrote. When this happens, as it sometimes does, we may protest vigorously or fret in private but editors will merely shrug or be sincerely apologetic. Whether you obtain an apology or not, unless legal issues are at stake, there is no way of unwriting what has been published – and this is a hard lesson for some writers to learn.

Not long ago I read the list of corrections *The New Yorker* was obliged to print following errors in a 1995 geographical agent and broker listing given a week earlier:

Aberdeen is in Scotland, not Saudi Arabia or England. Antwerp is in Belgium, not Barbados. Belfast is in Northern Ireland, not Nigeria. Cardiff is in Wales, not Vietnam. Edinburgh is in Scotland, not England. Helsinki is in Finland, not Fiji. Moscow is in Russia, not Qatar.

I wonder how many heads rolled after that!

There are two sides to every coin and happiness is surely finding the very book you want on your own doorstep when you aren't even looking for it. Are you a car-boot sale addict? A jumble sale frequenter? A charity shop casual? A school fete family? I've picked up just what I wanted in all these places. Often what I found wasn't on my prepared list of 'books I badly need or must have' but proved to be a useful addition to it, leading me into new and profitable avenues of research that hadn't previously occurred to me. Many and wonderful are the bargains I've found at such events; they are excellent value in the money sense and have often proved *invaluable* in their use to me. Do you, like me, avidly pore over piles of books friends or neighbours might throw out when they spring-clean or move house? Never miss an opportunity to add to your store of books for research!

Electronic help

Any writer with a computer and a telephone can communicate simply and immediately without having to involve any intermediaries. In non-technical language for those new to the world of computers, it simply means joining your telephone to your computer via a little box called a modem (a MOdulator DEModulator, for the technically-minded) so that the information you seek appears on the screen in front of you. All this is done with your computer keyboard and you don't touch the telephone at all. You can then save the information on disk, print it on paper and do whatever you like with it. Using this setup, *'e-mail'* (short for 'electronic mail') is a method of sending and receiving messages directly from one computer to another. No matter where you are in the world, proving you have a computer (just an ordinary home-user's machine) and a modem, I can send messages to you and you can reply to me. The messages are passed at lightning speed along the phone lines and appear on the screens in front of us – as well as being stored for future reading. The speed of transmitting messages (and information of any kind) depends on the rate at which the modem operates and can be breathtaking: the electronic network common to almost all universities can send the equivalent of the *Encyclopedia Britannica* along optical cables in just four seconds. The Internet is an extension of the same system and no further hardware is required to find yourself in a world you may come to think of as a researcher's dream. It can be of inestimable value to writers and the demands of each new writing project will determine just how and how much you use it.

If you are unsure about taking the plunge into the electronic world you may be able to try your hand in one of the 'cybercafes' set up in many towns large and small. There is even one in a little village near mine – and it is always busy. For a small extra charge on your cup of coffee you can experiment with the Internet on their equipment and get practical help at the same time. It can be quite an eye-opener!

When you've decided to join you 'enrol' as a customer of a specialist agency which organises all the complex links to join your computer at home with a vast global network, and once joined you leave all the technicalities to the agency. There are several such agencies, or 'access-providers', most of which charge a once-only joining fee (generally around £20 or £25). You can tap into news, general information, stock market prices, sport, train timetables and literally thousands of other topics; every day more are being added to the pool. The only costs thereafter are a small monthly sum (£10 or so per month is usual) which will only increase if you spend a really long time on-line each month, and your normal telephone bill.

The Internet provides four main services:

Firstly, it offers rapid direct communication with other people as an alternative to writing to them (which takes a couple of days, at best, to gain a response), trying to reach them by telephone when they're just too busy to give you their attention or sending faxes which may go unheeded. *E-mail* lets you 'write' to someone with a query or a request for information and receive a reply on your screen at almost unbelievable speed.

If you have questions but don't know the names or *e-mail* addresses of folk likely to know the answers, there are literally hundreds of thousands of people out there waiting to help you. All you have to do is to join (with a single button click) an appropriate group or conference or listing from the thousands offered to you, ask your question into the ether and wait for some obliging people to come back with a reply right on your screen. They surely will: the only problem facing you then might be you have far to much information from too many willing helpers! Should you wish to stop work in the midst of this research at your keyboard – do so. One of the great advantages of electronic research is the 'store and hold' service that waits till you next 'log on', i.e. switch your computer on again and begin another on-line session. This method of sending and receiving messages is ideal and cheap for very short letters or queries that might not justify the cost of a sheet of paper, an envelope and a stamp, or the delay that even the speediest first-class postal system can provide. Sending a letter or query of a few lines via your modem will add about five pence to your telephone bill! It can also be useful to have your messages and the replies you receive recorded for future reference on your hard disk; using this method, you can also receive and send computer artwork or graphics.

You can save on costs in several ways, one of the most useful being the facility to send a message to or ask a question of, say, a dozen people as quickly as you can send it to a single person. You want to ask more than a dozen? No problem – that's done just as easily and at enormous speed. As yet the Internet is not as widespread as are ordinary telephones, particularly at private addresses, nor does it reach as many people as 'snail-mail' but with *millions* of people worldwide joining the system every week it is simple for home-based writers to experience the ease and joys of being able to tap into the Internet resources.

The Internet's second use is for research and here it can prove invaluable. How much of your time and effort is occupied in getting to libraries or university archives or other places of reference? Get on the 'net' and give yourself a headstart. No more need the cost of research exceed what the copy will earn. From your own desk you merely tap into the records you wish to consult – and what you want appears on the screen in front of you. Actually such huge amounts of material are available that an early problem is how to find the wood for the trees; but the whole system is built with an easy-to-follow series of pointers to help you get to where you want to be with the minimum of fuss at the maximum rate. To be sure I wasn't going to exaggerate this point and mislead readers of this book I timed a question-and-answer session between myself, at my home in the UK, and a specialist university conference in Berkeley, California. Most universities the world over have many of their papers available for 'downloading'. I asked a question (about a particular breed of cat, as it happened) and received an immediate reply inviting me to expand my question, which I did. Back came two files of data and a list of more that I was unaware of and could have for the asking. I *e-mailed* back requesting another data file and was rewarded with all the information I could possibly need plus offers of further information from another source. The time taken for all this Atlantic crisscrossing? Three minutes, of which just one minute 42 seconds' worth, costing less than eight pence, would be added to my phone bill – with, as in any exchange of mail, the US contacts paying their own 'postage' costs.

Thirdly, if you just want more information but do not know a specific source that might help, you can 'log on' to any of the thousands of mailing lists or 'conferences' which are special-interest groups maintained by other people also engrossed in your topic. (A bonus: log on to a selection of these conferences and you'll never run dry of ideas.)

Lastly, you can use pages on the Internet as markets for your own copy. Most leading newspaper and magazine companies now publish electronic magazines (*e-zines*) so you sell your work to them and get paid for doing so – but that's another story. (See 'Rights' later in this book on page 160.)

As for those acronyms spattering any Internet talk – they're mostly simple software programs your computer uses to help you find your way round. For instance, WWW (World Wide Web) is almost like an incredibly detailed travel guide which not only tells you what the sights are at each location, but how to get there. USENET resembles a gigantic noticeboard split into many thousands of subjects. People (via their computers) just drop in, collect some snippets from the areas they are interested in and go away again. And I do stress the need to 'go away again', which means opt out of that particular field of interest and is easily accomplished at the click of your mouse. However beguiling all the information that comes you way might appear to be, there is frequently too much for your immediate and practical needs and too much can slow you down.

All major universities and many colleges and schools in the UK are connected to the academic network known as JANET (Joint Academic Network) where typical conferences are weather forecasts, book reviews, support for your particular make of printer, rugby football in Afghanistan (yes, really!), stock market prices, cooking with herbs – the scope is enormous and apparently without end.

But a word of caution! While it seems churlish to put a damper on the wonders of on-line help – which are numerous – I must remind you of the dangers. Thoroughly-researched information is a valuable commodity and few contacts will release it free of charge onto the Internet if they are making their living selling it, so be wary of assuming everything you find is wholly reliable. The extent to which you can trust what appears on your screen often depends on what it is you're looking for. I have found Internet research excellent in some instances but poor in others. Consider who it is who is prepared to distribute free information, and why. Authoritative sources may be fine but trusting information on Web pages may be risky. Thousands of experts set up their own Web pages on virtually any topic under the sun *and thousands more who are not experts do the same*. I could set-up a Web page packed with information and discourse and pictures about the history and intricacies of needlecraft, for example, with masses of 'relevant' information. How could you be certain I knew what I was talking about?

So my warning is this: use the Internet to get ideas, to give you background and a general 'feel', but for serious research always verify your sources.

Joining a writers' circle on-line is simple and fun and may be the answer to anyone wanting to 'meet' other writers but who cannot travel to a conventional circle of like-minded people. And because being on-line means the world is your oyster you may find a circle congenial to you actually has its base (or at least its most active members) on the other side of the world.

Even without joining the on-line world computer users greatly benefit from electronic research. It is not only quick and simple but also offers huge quantities of data in very small packages: the entire Bible, for instance, is easily stored on two or three low-resolution floppy disks available to the most basic computer-user.

CD-ROM

Another technique involves a format known as CD-ROM (Compact Disks with Read-Only-Memory). These look just like audio disks but are electronically developed to hold vast amounts of reference data. Although they only work with a special disk drive (a simple and not expensive addition to your computer if one is not already built-in) the cost of instant, accurate and almost unbelievably wide-ranging source material is quickly defrayed when compared to the time and money spent in traditional research methods away from one's desk. A single compact disk can hold over 600 Megabytes of data, roughly the equivalent of *quarter of a million* A4 pages, and this enormous capacity for storing information makes them potentially revolutionary research tools. There is no doubt the use of CD-ROMs makes light work of consulting any works of reference that would take up walls or even *rooms* of shelf space. Using interactive sound and vision for the first time from a CD-ROM can be quite a surprise: if you prefer to work in quietness you simply turn off the extra levels of multimedia sophistication you don't want.

Research help on CDs is equally simple. For rapid results try the *OED Encyclopedia* or *Grolier's Encyclopedia* which carries ten million words in 33,000 articles, 3,000 photos, 300 maps, 150 sounds and 85 video clips. Locate a precise reference anywhere on the disk in a matter of seconds at the touch of a key and choose how the results are displayed – alphabetically, chronologically, by frequency etc – on your screen, instantaneously. Isn't technology marvellous?

6
The spice of life

An editor I once worked for referred to a small band of his most useful writers as IDAs. This stood for 'I'll Do Anything' and you can be sure the IDAs were always popular. They also enjoyed a richer and more varied writing life than many of those doing the same type of job for successive editions – and they were well rewarded for their versatility. Are you an IDA? This chapter delves into many ways of broadening your experience by writing more than just articles. What else do you turn to in a magazine's pages? What are those unusual or intriguing bits readers so enjoy? Who writes or compiles them? An IDA? *You?*

Making your own corner

Some of the topics we discuss here refer to pieces published regularly in magazines. A crossword, a chess column, word puzzles, nature notes, competitions, book reviews; establish yourself as a contributor of such copy and the editor is likely to offer you a regular spot in the magazine. 'Village corner', 'This month's bird', 'Famous railway engines', 'Notable men of the county' – the opportunities are bounded only by your imagination.

Whatever your idea, try writing half a dozen sample pieces for your eyes only before approaching an editor. There are several important questions to answer in private and 'Will I run out of ideas for my corner?' is only one of them, although it is the most important. Before agreeing to a weekly, fortnightly, monthly or even quarterly commitment ask yourself if you can you keep to a deadline. Think carefully about your answer. For many years I have been a regular contributor of specialised copy to a variety of publications and I know from woeful personal experience that Heaven must almost fall before non-delivery or even lateness of copy can be excused. A friend came to stay? You've been too busy? Your typewriter or word-processor broke down? Too bad. But the rest of the world still goes about its business and magazines cannot afford to wait for you. Despite this, take heart:

editors, tough as they have to be to keep their periodicals afloat, are not entirely soulless. If you are *really* ill or face some dire crisis and you cannot keep to a deadline, let the editor know as soon as possible and he will see someone else does the work instead. Just don't let this happen too often or strain his forbearance too far! As usual, part of the solution to this problem is to be well-prepared, and if your speciality spot is one that does not rely on topicality, you should always see you have plenty of spare copy put by, for just such a 'rainy day'.

Children's pages

Women writers no longer have virtual monopoly of magazine pages published specially for children and I know of several men who do the job. When I was a young mother with small children I regularly read *Mother & Baby*, a parents' magazine. At the time it contained nothing specially aimed at pleasing the children of readers. If children had a part of this magazine, I mused, with pictures to colour and puzzles to work out, they would urge their mothers to buy it in preference to others of a similar type. I set to work.

With the invaluable help of an artist friend I produced enough copy and artwork for six consecutive issues. Then I wrote to the editor suggesting my planned column might suit her. I had softened her up by contributing plenty of copy to her pages in earlier months, and had (of course) always been quick to alter or amend anything at her request. Would she now give me a regular page for children? Yes, she would.

The job was better than I had dared to hope: would I, asked the editor, take a whole page every month with occasional spreads of two or three pages several times a year, to give the children a real part of the magazine? Would I! The page began as a Club for children to join. They received colourful badges which I bought for them from a leading manufacturer, and were offered a variety of competitions carefully designed for them. When I invited young readers to contact me the response was so great my small local sub-Post Office had to recruit extra sorters. Children wrote from all over this country and even from abroad. Success made me work very hard and involved a lot of activity, from meeting toy manufacturers (who supplied me with competition prizes) and companies producing babywear to interviewing groups of young mothers and infant teachers at play groups and arranging special treats for readers on selected occasions.

The job continued through three editorial changes and the stimulus of holding down a lively regular job taught me a great deal; it certainly helped develop and extend my writing skills for during this time I was also able to take on several other specialist columns of totally different types. Many tasks I undertook on *Mother & Baby* and on other titles taught me more about magazine production and I was able to spread my net wider still. So whatever type of column you would like to secure, it is only sensible to set about getting it in a methodical and professional manner.

There are few things more satisfying than having your own corner/column/page published regularly. Your name becomes known as a specialist contributing editor, which helps you sell work to other editors, and readers feel you are an important part of the magazine – which you are. Receiving letters, yes even problems, from them is surely the most genuine sign of approval for any writer.

Word puzzles

Word puzzles are popular attractions for readers in many magazines. The complexity and nature of published puzzles will reflect the readership and market study answers questions about what kind of word puzzle to compile. There are magazines exclusively devoted to word puzzles and on the whole those published are agreeably undemanding involving nothing more than locating words written in straight lines horizontally, vertically or diagonally in a grid of individual letters. There is virtually no skill required in either devising or solving such puzzles. This being so, the rewards for compilers are small.

If your market is of a specialist interest let the puzzle embrace words relevant to the jargon of the magazine, i.e. boating terms for a sailing magazine or cycling language for one for cyclist readers, adding a 'specially made' flavour to the puzzle as well as making it simpler for the readers to solve. Seasonal puzzles are also popular. This is an easy way to make such a word puzzle:

1 List at least a dozen appropriate words; up to 50 or 60 if the magazine is agreeable.

2 Draw a grid of the required size on squared paper.

3 Write two of the longest words at any position in the grid, interconnecting with a common letter and repeat this as many times as you can, using words not already on your list if necessary.

4 Continue placing words anywhere in the grid until you have used all on your list.

5 Use a different colour pen, at this stage, to write any letters you like in the blank spaces not used by your 'proper' words.

6 Check that all the words on your list (which will be printed beside the puzzle) exactly match those appearing in the puzzle (that also means being careful not to insert unintentional words when you fill in the blank spaces).

7 Make two top copies of the completed puzzle: one for publication and the other, on which you should circle the listed words, for the editor to try for himself. He won't publish it if you've made any mistakes!

Compiling more challenging word puzzles is fun. For several years I made occasional contributions to a well-known women's magazine's fascinating and highly specialised word-puzzle. It consisted of a number of words to be fitted into an irregular crossword pattern; both the words and the pattern varied each month. Although I never discovered how many entries my puzzles were expected to attract I was told that if the numbers fell below 'a minimum figure' they would be rejected. On two occasions they were returned as 'unsuitable' and this kept me on my toes – although it gave me a horrid jolt at the time. No doubt I had fallen into the trap of enjoying a particular writing job so much I had temporarily forgotten its purpose: to entertain and intrigue readers in large numbers. Enjoy what you are writing by all means but never let personal satisfaction take precedence over the hard facts of marketing reality. Enjoyment is a bonus.

Crosswords

Many magazines print crosswords and a good many others would like to do so if they could find compilers to provide what they want. Clearly magazines in the latter category are well worth studying. Children's magazines, trade and lesser-known journals are often keen to buy and submissions to these markets are not numerous, giving you a better chance if you are a beginner at crossword-compiling.

If you've ever tried you've probably found writing a few words in a bare block without any clear idea of where you're going or what you're doing soon leads to a 'block' of quite another sort – and defeat. A few precepts work wonders:

1 Construct a squared block complete with 'blacks'. Copy one from elsewhere if you wish (copyright resides in clues, not empty blocks) or devise your own. Symmetry is satisfying though not vital but all words must interconnect.

2 Make a list of words that might feature in the complete puzzle; words suitable to the publication, its readers and the language they share.

3 Fill the block with words (see below).

4 Number squares in the block where the solution words are to be entered.

5 Write your clues and number them to match the numbers in the block.

Item (3) is, of course, the most difficult part: 'fill the block with words' sounds easy until you start doing it. Three tips known to experienced compilers are useful:

a) The letters E, T, A, O, I, N and S (the most commonly used in the English language) are the best with which to begin words.
b) Words with few vowels sit more happily on the left of the block, especially at the top, than elsewhere.
c) Be wary about abbreviations, plurals and words ending with vowels other than E.

Compiling crosswords can be addictive and there is no precise list of rules that will make it simple because each crossword is unique. But this is one area where, even if perfection at times seems bafflingly elusive, practice does make perfect. And that is the only solution.

Book reviewing

This is the goal of many writers, especially those who imagine reviewing books means reading what you like, at your own pace, and then getting handsomely paid for writing about it. Alas, it doesn't.

Certainly book reviewing for magazines is a task writers enjoy but consider the following:

1 Reviewers must be well read with a wide and varied knowledge of published books. You cannot intelligently comment on a new book if you cannot 'see' it in its context or *genre*.

2 A review is not merely a summary of the book's story or contents. Its purpose is to tell readers, with your justification, why it is (or is not) of interest and delight.

3 Discipline and accuracy are essential. Power-hungry, name-dropping or revenge-seeking reviewers are unemployable.

4 Reviewers are hired for their experience. Gaining it takes perseverance and patience.

5 It's a time-consuming job. Skimming through chapter headings or rewriting the blurb will not suffice.

6 Even high-circulation magazines pay comparatively lowly fees.

If you are determined to be a published book reviewer try your hand with small circulation, perhaps local, magazines. You will have to buy the books in the first place and may not get paid much, if anything, for reviewing them but you will have made a start. The reviews will be useful to show editors higher up the publishing ladder when you seek a regular reviewing corner of your own in an established magazine and the writing of them will boost your confidence. Practising how to write briefly and concisely is valuable and book reviews are generally short, seldom exceeding five hundred words. Consumer magazines receive quantities of books from publishers eager for the publicity a review can bring and when you work as a regular reviewer the decision of which books to select for review may be made by the features or page editor, or it may even be left in your hands.

And what is the question asked most frequently by eager potential book reviewers? Yes, become an established magazine reviewer and you do keep the books.

Magazine competitions

When I won a cash prize in a consumer magazine competition sponsored by *Heinz* I fell to thinking how well the competition was attuned to likely readers, how popular it must have been and how I could devise different competitions to interest the editor for future issues.

In due course I worked out several competitions of a similar standard and appeal to those already published and began a careful courtship of the editor involved. Would he be interested in seeing what I had to offer? Yes. Could I send or show him some

I thought he would like? Yes, but with no promises on his part. Then, when he'd had a chance to consider my submissions a correspondent wrote to the editor asking for a greater variety of competitions to enter. He replied to me – with acceptance of all my competitions, wanting to publish them in successive monthly editions of his magazine. Would I visit him at Head Office to discuss with some of his suppliers just how the competitions were to be administered?

This led to a pleasant little writing job that could have lasted longer than it did had not other more pressing work intervened. It's a task I gladly recommend to any writer with more than a passing interest in entering or compiling competitions as there are many agreeable side-effects. The contests may be simple quizzes but they often take the form of a few questions and answers (generally about the sponsored product) followed by a sentence-completion task. This might be something like 'I love Blogg's Cereal because ... ' or entrants may be asked to list in preferred order a number of attributes of a particular cleaning product or a company selling cut-price holidays.

Sometimes magazines run competitions with big prizes as definite reader-magnets. These also serve reader-research purposes, the responses giving the publishers an idea into what readers want and in what numbers. These competitions may also be the work of outside contributors, especially those known to have experience in this field.

Editors are always open to competition suggestions but be sure to do all your thinking before making your initial approach: there are many points to be settled. Is your proposed competition to be solved by luck, perseverance, knowledge, or with what combination of the three? There are legal niceties to be observed even in such an apparently innocent pastime as setting competitions. Is the solution to be printed on another page in the same issue or are there to be prizes for submitting the correct solution? Where will the prizes come from? Who will judge the entries and despatch the prizes?

Once in the competition frame of mind you may like to enter a few trade contests yourself. Forms are generally freely available in large supermarkets or in the magazines available at their check-out counters. This is good training in writing with economy and aptness and can be highly profitable. I know people who have won cars, overseas holidays and even houses just by completing sentences in a few suitable words. Will you be the next to do so?

Arts and entertainment

Do you love music, fine art, theatre or films? All entertainment organisers crave publicity and that means editors may be willing to consider previews of forthcoming events. Regional magazines, for instance, are often happy to preview drama or arts presentations soon to occur in their areas. A particular play may be scheduled for the local Opera House or the work of a much-acclaimed artist will shortly be on show at a nearby Art Gallery. If you have good contacts in the theatre or arts world you could be just the person to write magazine previews. As usual, contact the editor with your credentials (you are not likely to make much progress without any as this is seldom a field for complete beginners) and ask if he is interested. This job attracts competition, not least because of free tickets and allied perks, so your first task may be not be covering a very sophisticated event but it will give you experience for when greater challenges come your way.

To write a preview of a particular event you must ensure your copy is directed to an issue of the magazine with a specific date on it (known as a 'dated issue'). When it is important to tie-in your copy with a particular date mention this point clearly in your covering letter even if it has been fully discussed with the editor prior to submission.

Fillers

The widespread and almost universal use of modern technology has revolutionised the technique of laying out magazine pages. With a few simple key strokes columns can be moved, headings resized, pix cropped and everything adapted to suit the page editor's precise requirements. The results can look neater and better than in the old pre-tech days but the change has not been without casualties. With everything so easily lined up to fill its allotted space, those little gaps so useful for small fillers have virtually disappeared. All the same, we writers can turn this apparent loss to our advantage by upgrading small items – old 'filler' material – into snippets meriting a dignity and place of their own.

You like verse? Short quotations in 'boxed' format (that simply means submitting them enclosed inside a ruled box) can add variety to pages rather heavy on text and are popular as regularly published items.

Palindromes fascinate me. Do they do the same for other people? Yes, I discovered when I started a running-filler on the

topic in a general interest magazine. I wrote a short and deliberately provocative item quoting the longest palindrome I could
find at the time:

ABLE WAS I ERE I SAW ELBA

Did anyone know a longer one? Entries flooded in and over the
next few issues my original 19 letter sample grew to:

TO PREDICATE GO GET A CIDER POT (25 letters)

and:

TO CLARET ALAS IT IS A LATERAL COT (27 letters)

I thought this must be the end of the line, but no. An enterprising
reader clinched it with:

SATAN OSCILLATE MY METALLIC SONATAS (an incredible
31 letters)

At the same time I introduced date palindromes. Ordinary ones
are quite common and I reminded readers that, for instance, the
29th of every month in 1992 (except October and December)
reads backwards as well as forwards: 29-4-92, 29-6-92 etc. But
there was something extra about the 18th of January in 1981. This
was a superpalindrome year and 18-1-81 not only read the same
backwards as forwards but (in suitably written figures) upside
down as well. The same happened in August (18-8-81) and
November (18-11-81) that year. Who, I invited readers, could
work out what the next superpalindromic date would be? The
response was not long in coming[1] and the whole topic provoked
lively letters the editor.

With that he decided to call a halt. I use the term 'running-
filler' because that's exactly what it was; the topic soon running
out of steam when readers who wanted to contribute had done
so and there was nothing further to add. (Of course if you know
any palindromes longer than 31 letters ...)

Quotations both serious and humorous can also lighten a
page. A colleague contributed an amusing or clever quotation to
a weekly magazine for five or six years under the title 'I wish I'd
said ...' And children's sayings never fail to bring smiles to
readers' lips.

Humour is always welcome providing it is suited to the taste
and style of the magazine. I've found bits and pieces that have

[1] January 10th 2001: 10-1-01.

come my way well worth jotting down for use as filler material. Like these:

> Seen on the noticeboard of a Northumbrian golf club: *'The ladies section will be glad to play the gentlemen when they have nothing on.'*

> From a weekly newspaper: *'John and Mary would like to thank family, friends and neighbours for the presents, cards and flowers received on the arrival of their twin daughters. We would also like to thank the vicar for making it all possible.'*

To a writer, nothing heard, read or seen is ever wasted and even the smallest titbits can be put to good use.

Writers of fillers and letters will find a wealth of practical help in a useful little book written especially for them. *Letters and Fillers* by Frances Coombes (Niche Publications London, PO Box 3131, London NW5 4DW) is a marketing guide for people who want to write for publication and payment. It details the needs of 50 popular magazines and newspapers and embraces different types of filler and letters.

Letters to the editor

I'm sad when I hear some writers saying writing letters to the editor, letters for publication, is a waste of time. 'It's the last resort,' they sigh, 'because they won't pay me anything even if my letters are published.' There are at least two faults in such despairing argument. Far from being the last resort of the otherwise unpublished, writing a letter to the editor focuses the mind on a single aspect of a single theme and is a valuable exercise in the twin disciplines of conciseness and relevance. Nor is it always unpaid as the many dedicated letter writers to magazines will confirm. Perhaps, by the very nature of their self-imposed task, we should consider such enterprising and busy folk to be following a hobby while 'proper' writers engaged in work of greater substance than letters-to-the-editor prefer to think of themselves in more serious vein. But what's the difference? Whatever the length, weight or subject matter of our end-product and wherever it appears in a magazine's editorial pages it is a valid piece of published work of which we may be proud.

Those wishing to write letters to the editor need to study their intended markets as closely as anyone writing longer pieces. Brevity is essential with as few as fifty words often the average length of published letters. You need to make your mark without any preamble and encompass all you want to say in the word limit allowed or your most important point may be cut. (And that means, of course, the letter won't be published at all.)

Imagine reading a magazine and finding a letter-to-the-editor that you simply must read out to those around you; perhaps it makes you laugh or annoys you or confirms your opinion about something or evokes happy memories or gives you some information you need or comments on something you read in last week's issue. These are the types of letters that are published and the sort you could be submitting for publication. You may get paid (magazines usually indicate their intentions, sometimes only paying for the best published at the time) or you may receive some small present in thanks. Frequently general and women's titles offer gifts or cash payments for the best letter received by a certain date and written about a specified topic. This, of course, is one of the many editorial ploys to encourage regular purchase.

When editors invite you to give your own views or relate your experiences you can be sure it is not just to assure themselves of a swollen postbag: it is another of the publisher's methods of researching into what his readers want and discovering what sort of people they are. What could be more direct than the invitation to 'write and tell us'? Make your reply one of those chosen for publication and both you and the editor are happy. Whether you are paid in cash or kind, or not at all, if your letter is published in a mass-selling periodical or a small one in the area where you live one reward probably coming your way is the response from other readers – and that is always worth having.

Resist letting success in this field go to your head. Give editors the suspicion you are engaging in writing letters as more than just an interested and observant reader of their publication (you might, horror, even be making a part-time job out of it) and they could turn your offerings away with nary a glance. The answer is to write letters that editors know other readers will like reading and to cast your net wide. The wider you spread it the more your market-study will extend and the sounder your judgement of markets will be for submitting other work.

When you're known . . .

When you've achieved success with some of the challenges above you will find you enjoy being an IDA. But the most exciting task comes when you are asked to stand in for an absent staff member. It always pays to watch out for the pregnant! In due course there's bound to be a gap on the staff, a vacancy sure to last some months, and an IDA is the ideal person to fill it. Such an arrangement can suit all parties: the editor, who knows he can rely on you and your work, the absent staff member who can take time off without feeling she has left her colleagues floundering, and you, who have been hoping for an opportunity to spread your wings.

Other staff absences due to holidays or illness present chances for the enterprising freelance who has shown all the important IDA qualities. And sometimes absent staff, for a number of reasons, don't come back ...

Further afield

Most writing tasks have a happy knack of leading to others, which makes the whole business so satisfactory. Turn your eyes to further assignments outside the business of magazines. Here are ten off-beat writing jobs worth pursuing:

1 writing company histories for local firms;
2 advertising features for area or regional newspapers;
3 brochures and leaflets for hotels, holiday or coach companies;
4 charity appeals for fund-raisers;
5 notices and posters for schools and libraries;
6 booklets for walkers and owners of historic houses;
7 speeches for public figures who are not writers;
8 CVs for job-seekers;
9 preparing company internal and annual reports, editing in-house magazines, compiling publicity material and anniversary brochures;
10 preparing applications for people seeking grants etc.

Using your imagination

A writer I know in North Wales has a passion for short verses of the type often found in greetings cards. She collects them in albums under various headings: children, nostalgia, animals and pets, the countryside and so on. One day when she was thumbing through her collection she thought she could write verses equally acceptable to card recipients if not better. She took note of the publishers' names on the back of the cards and began researching a wider field. A friend suggested she should contact

The Greetings Card Association (41 Links Drive, Elstree, Herts WD6 3PP) for a list of members who accept freelance verses and she now sees her own verses appearing regularly in greetings cards of all types. She has made a hobby that interests her into a small part-time occupation bringing in a some welcome cheques.

Could you be an IDA? Of all writers they probably have the most fun.

7
Overseas markets

The concept of market study remains paramount in importance when selling to markets overseas, while obtaining copies of titles to study is often a difficulty. Friends and relations in distant countries should be encouraged to send you copies or bring them to you on their travels. If this is unsuccessful, write and ask the magazine to send you some back numbers, being sure, of course, to include International Reply Coupons sufficient to cover the cost of the wanted titles and their postage. The cover prices quoted will be in their currency so remember to check the operative exchange rate. And don't send envelopes for return bearing UK stamps to countries that do not use them. Not only is this wasteful, it tells the receiving editor you have little knowledge of the country you hope to sell to: hardly the best impression to give when you are trying to make a sale.

Submitting copy totally 'out of the blue' without any prior contact is generally a waste of time and effort. This is not always so – but why make things harder for yourself than they need be? Now electronic contact is as easy across half the world as to the next street, it is a simple matter to *e-mail* your chosen title – wherever in the world it may be. (See Chapter 5: Electronic help.)

When you submit copy be clear about the rights you are offering. An increasing number of American titles ask for All Rights. This means anything already sold in this or any other country will not be acceptable. Although this practice can be restrictive, for work that is easily adapted for other markets, i.e. rewritten, or is unlikely to sell elsewhere, the higher fees usually offered for All Rights sales may be welcome.

Curiosity about other people and the way they live is the life-blood of writers all over the world. This is keenly recognised by magazine publishers overseas who welcome acceptable freelance submissions from other countries simply because they are different. Infertility, for instance, knows no national or international boundaries yet an article on dealing with it written for, let us say, an American magazine by a British writer will certainly take a different viewpoint from one written by an American. It's not that one will necessarily be better than the other but that, in the case of writing for overseas publications, distance lends the enchantment of looking through new eyes. Don't let's forget reality; enchantment is fine, but in the previous paragraph the word 'acceptable' is more important. In selling internationally all the parameters of market study obtain and if you don't want to waste time, effort and money on winging unwanted words round the world it is vital to observe them.

Most foreign Embassies in the UK are happy to provide information about magazines published in their countries; I give relevant addresses below and *Whitaker's Almanack* and other reference books detail more in countries not covered in this chapter. In every case it is advisable to discover the correct name of your contact as most overseas markets appreciate the personal touch. But also remember the holders of positions on magazines may change and as the time lapse between your enquiry and eventual submission will probably take longer than the same procedure would here, address your intended recipient by a job title as well as a personal name. For topical or timed articles you want to appear in a magazine on a particular date, work backwards from it to choose when to post your copy. Most overseas magazines work to publishing time schedules similar to those observed in this country but it is wise to exceed them. So for an article you hope the editor will accept for publication in the July edition, say, of his monthly title, you should post your copy by Christmas if not before. This will allow ample time for him to contact you about anything that might arise: queries, requests for elucidation or expansion on particular points, further information, pictures or anything else he might want.

Of course your market study will take note of your potential title's special interests and likely (or stated) taboos but always supply overseas periodicals with the very best service you can provide. All your copy must offer First Rights of the country you are submitting to. That still means your article may have been published in the UK, selling First British Rights, but no others. As European trade develops magazine publishers are talking of merging the reproduction rights of several countries under a single 'European' label. Already some organisations market 'pan-European' titles, i.e. the same magazines sold in their own languages, sometimes with different titles, in several EU countries. But national differences in what readers want make this less easy than it sounds and, with some specialised exceptions, virtually all copy originally written for publication in one country needs rewriting before it is acceptable in another. Notwithstanding this (which we writers can hardly consider a problem) there is sure to be a significant increase in the pan-European method of marketing and I recommend writers with an eye on regular future sales to follow its development; the problems will be solved, because that is the only reason problems exist, and we cannot be far from the time when contributors simply deliver copy to their nearest office – in their home country – to submit to titles in as many European countries as participate in the scheme.

Market study of international magazines extends to finding out as much as you can about the country you wish to submit to. For general information about a country the Department of Trade and Industry's guides provide valuable background reading; copies are free and obtainable on request from any of the DTI's regional offices or from 1 Victoria Street, London SW1H 0ET.

Never forget the golden rule of marketing: you are writing for readers not editors or publishers. Anything that helps you understand who those readers are and what sort of lives they lead must be beneficial. So don't skimp reader-research; that is what we must follow with quality writing.

Payment varies enormously, is not always listed in reference guides and should be ascertained before submission. Even magazines paying little are generally worth dealing with, particularly at the start of your writing career. They sometimes present opportunities to expand overseas sales to higher paying markets in due course. Low-paying markets also attract less competition than the high-payers; only you can decide how much your copy is worth in terms of cash profit, so you may have to balance the expense of mailing overseas with the less easily costed advantages of gaining a foothold at the bottom of the ladder.

Some magazines, particularly in the US, furnish writers with an advanced list of themes to be covered in forthcoming issues. These are enormously helpful and can save fruitless effort in the preparation of copy on a topic already in the pipeline. They also provide useful extra guidance to market requirements, reflecting considered editorial policy.

The language

If you write only in your mother tongue international markets need not be barred to you. In general there are four methods of

selling overseas and whichever you choose the language
problem is easily overcome. I outline them below in my personal
order of preference:

1 Do-it-yourself

This involves doing all the work yourself, including market
study, querying potential editors and selling to them as well as
researching, writing and presenting your copy, with illustrations
if required. You may be asked to contribute to translation costs or
even to meet them in full. But sometimes, depending on the
status and strength of the market, the receiving magazine bears
all such expenses. There are undoubted advantages in a do-it-
yourself approach not least of which is that all the proceeds are
yours. More importantly, nothing quite replaces the personal
touch and working this way may establish what could be valuable future contacts. But you do have to be patient as finding the
right market can be a lengthy process. You also have to bear all
the costs.

2 Hands across the sea

Find a friend in your targeted country to help and share the
burdens of market research and postal expenses. Someone with
knowledge or at least interest in the writing business will be most
helpful and the ideal person could be a writer trying to sell to
markets in this country. A good friend can save you time and
money there but don't forget the time and money you will have
to expend on your friend's copy here. When your friend can tell
you of markets not listed in any guidebook, never written about
in writers' magazines, virtually unknown here and yet longing
for freelance copy of the very type you want to write – when that
happens this method of selling overseas beats all others. Maybe
your friend can also help if translation into another tongue is
involved. But perfect fluency is essential, as any professional
translator will tell you, so be careful before accepting such an
offer. Inadequate translation can ravage all your hard work and
will inevitably spoil what might have been a valuable friendship.

3 Syndication

This can be the least troublesome way to sell overseas and frees
you from any translation problems. If you just want to concentrate on writing and let someone else cope with marketing and all
its associated time-consuming tasks this is the way to work. Lists
of syndication agents are to be found in the *Writers' & Artists'*

Yearbook but it pays to be sure of the terms of agencies before handing over your work. They also vary widely in translation fees; some charge a lot, others nothing, one may act promptly while another merely adds your copy to a heap gathering dust on the floor, and a few always announce your work needs rewriting – for a fee. Syndication agents generally prefer ideas to finished pieces and will sometimes wish to mould them – or tell you how to mould them – to suit their own predilections: as this can prove more trouble than it is worth (and often ends in tears) I do not advise entering into such an agreement. But if a syndication agent expresses interest in your suggested topic and its likely treatment you just write it up and hand it over. How can you distinguish the goodies from the baddies? There is nothing like the recommendation of a writing friend who has dealt with an agency you are hoping to use. Really good ones (and there are several) have sufficient clients already and may not be willing to accept any more. It is important to them that you should have plenty of copy to market and that you can keep it coming. The one-off article or even the just-now-and-then piece is unlikely to interest top-notch agencies when they have clients on their books who provide them with regular bread-and-butter. To succeed in syndication you should aim to be such a client.

4 Literary agents
Locate a literary agent who will do all the international marketing for you. Non-fiction writers will find this is not easy – and if you are without a proven track-record you may find it impossible. If you ask me, I think we freelance non-fiction writers do better without agents anyway.

Markets

The most reliable reference guide to markets both national and international is *Willing's Press Guide* (there is an overseas volume) but inevitably, being an annual publication, even the most recent edition is out-of-date before it reaches your hands. This fact highlights the importance of personal market study, for which there is no substitute, lists and guidebooks (even this one) notwithstanding.

In these pages it is only possible to give details of a few overseas markets in a handful of countries but perhaps that is no disadvantage for freelances. Any less-than-comprehensive list has to be selective, inevitably restricting some potential contributors and falsely encouraging others. I cannot know the writing ambitions and abilities of everyone reading this, so I mention the following markets with three injunctions:

1) details are published solely to whet the appetite;

2) in no way are they substitutes for personal market study and research;

3) market information is correct at the time I write this but may not still be so when you read it.

Some of the international magazines listed below (in country alphabetic order), with brief information, are not to be found in any conventional market guides: I just keep my eyes and ears open and follow the advice outlined above: it works!

Australia
(Australian High Commission, Australia House, Strand, London WC2B 4LA)
Standards of payment made by Australian magazines are generally modest but reports indicate the situation is improving. (Perhaps you might ask for more than you expect to receive or complain if what you are offered is too low to make it worthwhile submitting copy?) For serious marketing send for information from The Media, Entertainment and Arts Alliance, 360 King Street, West Melbourne, Australia, which offers services to freelance writers and proves very helpful in negotiating with editors and marketing. Members receive useful publications and newsletters.

The following may also provide beneficial information for writers wanting to sell to the Australian market.

1 Australian Society of Authors, 98 Pitt Street, Redfern, NSW 2016, Australia.
2 Australian Society of Travel Writers, PO Box 965, Neutral Bay, NSW 2089, Australia.
3 Australian Literature Board, 181 Lawson Street, Redfern, NSW 2016, Australia.

Australian Woman's Spirit
Upbeat magazine for women's enlightenment through a wide range of tools and ideas, offering support and inspiration to help self-awareness. Photos welcome. PO Box 146, Highbury, SA 5089, Australia.

Cleo
Looking for direct to-the-point features of 800-2,500 words. For single mid-twenties women, most published articles are about relationships, self-improvement, sex, friendship – with first-person reports, and celebrity interviews with an Australian connection. 54 Park Street, Sydney, NSW 2000, Australia.

Flirt
Frank and fun articles wanted about sex and relationships. Pix welcome. 180 Bourke Road, Alexandria, NSW 2015, Australia.

The Independent Monthly
The editor is always looking for well researched high quality articles. 4th Floor, 64 Kippax street, Surry Hills, NSW 2010, Australia.

New Woman
For modern liberated women aged 25-44. PO Box 279, North Sydney, NSW 2060.

Single Life
Aimed at single people, wants positive articles, humour welcome. 500-2,000 words. Suite 1, 254 Dandenong Road, East St Kilda, Victoria 3182, Australia.

Talk to Animals
Full colour glossy, wants upbeat factual articles from all over the world. Photos welcome. PO Box A305, Sydney South, NSW 2000, Australia.

Belgium
(Embassy of Belgium, 103 Eaton Square, London SW1W 9AB)

Knack
General information, the economy, sports, culture and politics for Dutch-speaking Belgium – see below. Research Park, 1731 Zellick, Belgium.

Le Vif/l'Express
News magazine for French-speaking Belgium, the counterpart of *Knack* (above) with features on general affairs, politics, the economy, culture and sports. 33 place de Jamblinne de Meux, 1040 Brussels, Belgium.

Canada
(Canadian High Commission, Macdonald House, 1 Grosvenor Square, London W1X 0AB)
The general library service at the Canadian High Commission was axed some years ago but the annual *Canadian Almanac & Directory* should be in any good reference library or, failing that, in the British Library. You may also find it helpful to contact the Canadian Writers Guide, 195 All State Parkway, Markham, Ontario L3R 4T8.

Most of the 1,000+ magazines published across the country are well-written and upbeat. The great US market is not far away so Canadian periodicals have to be tough to survive.

Canadian
The in-flight publication of Canadian Airlines International. Likes travel and business interest pieces 1000-15,000 words. Payment is on acceptance but varies. 111 Avenue Road, Suite 801, Toronto, Canada M5R 3J8.

Canadian Author
For Canadian writers of all ages at all levels of experience. 95% freelance written. Interviews, informative and how-to articles. 1,000-2,500 words. No personal, lightweight writing experiences or fillers. Send for sample copy and writer's guidelines. Suite 500, 275 Slater Street, Ottawa, Ontario, Canada K1P 5H9.

Canadian Biker Magazine
Family-orientated publication uniting Canadian motorcyclists from coast to coast through the dissemination of information in a non-biased open forum. Copy on new products, events, touring, racing, information from industry, interviews (Canadian subjects preferred), vintage and custom motorcycling. All submissions must include photographs/illustrations. The best writers for this market are likely to be closely involved with the motorcycle industry and wholly familiar with some aspect(s) of it. PO Box 4122, Victoria, British Columbia V8X 3X4, Canada.

Good Times
Published ten times a year for older and mostly retired readers. 1,000-1,500 words. Welcomes coloured slides. Write for sample copy and guidelines. 5148 St Lawrence Boulevard, Montreal, Quebec, Canada H2T 1R8.

Denmark
(Royal Danish Embassy, 55 Sloane Street, London SW1X 9SR)

Damernes Verden
This Danish title (in Danish) welcomes a variety of feature articles for women. Bonniers Specialmagasiner, Strandboulevarden 130, 2100 Koebenhavn OE., Denmark.

IN
Another women's magazine known to welcome freelance submissions. Bladforlaget, Vesterbrogade 16, 1506 Koebenhavn V., Denmark.

Euroman
A similar type publication as above, but for men. Klosterstraede 23, 1157 Koebenhavn K., Denmark.

France
(French Embassy, 58 Knightsbridge, Longon SW1X 7JT)
A small red book simply titled *FRANCE – a journalist's guide* is issued by the French Embassy's information department. It identifies a number of periodicals published in France, with titles, editorial addresses and phone numbers. This little book is, incidentally, a veritable treasure-chest of assorted material about France: its stated purpose is to present everyday information for use by English-speaking journalists. It contains over 1,500 addresses of government, political, economic, cultural and social organanisations, information on the media, sources of documentation, titles of reference books and practical and general statistics and information. A useful research tool.

Germany
(Embassy of the Federal Republic of Germany, 23 Belgrave Square, London SW1X 8PZ)
The German periodical publishing business is huge, second in the European Union only to our own, and magazines regularly accept copy written in almost any language from all over the world. Leading German magazines employ their own translators of anything they want to buy that is not written in German. As I write, the general translation fee (which writers are expected to pay) varies from £50 to £150 per thousand words. But if you throw your hands up in horror at this, remember that compared to the majority of British titles German magazines pay high fees: the equivalent of £400 per 1,000 words is not unusual.

Frau Im Spiegel
Published weekly for women aged from 20 to 45. Welcomes British tradition, royalty, celebrities etc. Dr Julius Leberstrasse 3-7, Luebeck, Germany. UK representative: Gruner & Jahr, 7 Cavendish Square, London W1M 9HA.

Das Neue Blatt
General interest weekly for older women, publishing a wide range of articles. Heinrich Bauer Verlag, Postfach 10 04 14, Burchardstrasse 11, W 2000, Hamburg 1.

Quick
Weekly in-depth periodical dealing with social, political, and moral issues of worldwide interest. Interviews and illustrations wanted. Postfach 20 17 28, 8000, Munchen 2.

Holland
(Royal Netherlands Embassy, 38 Hyde Park Gate, London SW7 5DP)
A high proportion of Dutch people read and speak English and many regularly read magazines published on both sides of the English Channel. There are many Dutch periodicals detailed in *Willings Press Guide*. The magazine business is thriving, sophisticated and comprehensive.

The Netherlander
Weekly publication in English for readers (and writers) on financial and economic affairs. Het Financieele Dagblad, PO Box 216, 1000 AE Amsterdam, The Netherlands.

Hong Kong
(Hong Kong Government Office, 6 Grafton Street, London W1X 3LB)

Discovery
This quality glossy monthly is the in-flight magazine for Cathay Pacific Airlines and is looking for freelance articles of 800-2,000 words on a wide range of subjects. Send a synopsis first. Feature sections include those devoted to music, motoring, food, history, sport and literature. Extra pay is offered for top quality photos. Emphasis (HK) Ltd, 505-508 Westlands Centre, 20 Westlands Road, Quarry Bay, Hong Kong.

Ireland
(Irish Embassy, 17 Grosvenor Place, London SW1X 7HR)
With so many tempting opportunities in European markets east-ward-looking freelance writers sometimes ignore the small but established Irish market. More than 120 titles are regularly published in the Republic, many of them catering for a variety of trades and (as in other countries) their themes cover a wide range of tastes. In any newsagent's shop you will find magazines catering for just about everyone with every interest: Irish life, sport, home and family, motoring, arts, the countryside – they're all there. But while glossy monthlies look good on the shelf and perhaps add an air of sophistication, the best sellers are generally at the cheaper end of the market. Nearly all of them are keen on buying from freelances who offer just what they want. The normal rules of market-research apply: dissect recent editions of potential targets and make thoughtful notes about their charac-teristics before deciding who the readers are, whether to write for a particular title, what you will write about, why your copy will capture readers and how you can sell the idea (and such convic-tion) to the editor before you write it.

The Furrow
Pastoral, social and religious articles published monthly. St Patrick's College, Maynooth, Co. Kildare, Eire.

Hot Press
Lively fortnightly publication wanting well-written stories on sport, music, religion, sex – and anything out-of-the-ordinary – to interest teenagers to 40-year olds. Pictures welcome. 13 Trinity Street, Dublin 2, Eire

IMAGE
A well-established glossy monthly published for leisured women with time and money to spend on their homes and families, and more especially on themselves. 22 Crofton Road, Dun Laoghaire, Co. Dublin, Eire.

Ireland of the Welcomes
A high proportion of American readers have helped keep this fine old bi-monthly flourishing for more than forty years – and this fact should help with market study. Bought mainly by postal subscription, it carries quality features with illustrations about many aspects of Ireland and the Irish, to boost tourism. Irish Tourist Board, Baggot Street Bridge, Dublin 2, Eire.

Ireland's Eye
Articles and features with an Irish flavour. Cartoons welcomed. Lynn Industrial Estate, Mullingar, Co. Westmeath, Eire.

Ireland's Own
The best known and probably most popular weekly for free-lances from both sides of the Irish Sea. Send a stamped self-addressed envelope for a recent copy and the editor's requirements. North Main Street, Wexford, Eire.

Irish Medical Times
A weekly publishing medical and humourous copy with a medical slant. 15 Harcourt Street, Dublin 2, Eire.

IT Magazine (Irish Tatler)
Published monthly to cover Irish interests in many parts of the country. General and women's interests particularly favoured. 126 Lower Baggot Street, Dublin 2, Eire.

Reality
Illustrated monthly for Christian living with articles on all aspects of modern life. Redemptorist Publications, Orwell Rd, Rathgar, Dublin 6, Eire.

U Magazine
Well-researched and well-written interviews, profiles and features are always welcomed by this lively title where submissions merely skimming the topic are not required. Smurfit Publications, 126 Lower Baggot St, Dublin 2, Eire.

Woman's Way
Ireland's largest circulation title for women with readership over a wide age range. A family-orientated human-interest magazine claiming to offer something for everyone. Smurfit Publications, 126 Lower Baggot St, Dublin 2, Eire.

The Word
Catholic illustrated monthly for the family. General interest and good picture features. Divine Word Missionaries, Maynooth, Co. Kildare, Eire.

New Zealand
(New Zealand High Commission, New Zealand House, London SW1Y 4TQ)

With a widely-scattered population of less than 4 million New Zealand supports a lively press including more than 600 magazines. They cover topics from accountancy to yachting and present excellent marketing opportunities to observant writers in the UK.

Bits & Bytes
Every month (except January) for computer users. PO Box 9870, Newmarket, Auckland, New Zealand.

Boating World
Features and pictures of New Zealand interest. Sail or power pleasure boating, how-to and technical articles welcomed. Private Bag 93209, Parnell, Auckland, New Zealand.

New Zealand Woman's Weekly
A popular weekly with some affinities to similar publications in the UK. Private Bag, Dominion Road, Auckland 3, New Zealand.

Straight Furrow
Published fortnightly, this farming publication has a wide readership. PO Box 715, Wellington, New Zealand.

South Africa
(High Commission of the Republic of South Africa, South Africa House, Trafalgar Square, London WC2N 5DP)

Drive
A monthly glossy wanting off-beat articles on anything to do with motoring. Copy should be well-written and about 1,000 words in length. Humour is welcome. PO Box 32083, Braamfontein, 2017, Johannesburg, South Africa.

Flying Springbok
An in-flight A4 glossy magazine given free to passengers on flights. Looking for travel articles but only those relating to places on South African Airways routes. High quality only, with photos. Send completed article straightaway; no initial synopses. PO Box 3734, Randburg, 2125, South Africa.

SA Sports Illustrated
Looking for short synopses of articles for sports fans, mainly men – profiles, interviews etc. PO Box 16386, Vlaeberg, 8018, Capetown, South Africa.

SA Yachting
Monthly glossy wanting work from experienced yachting writers mainly in Australia or New Zealand. High standard, perhaps technical or with a good knowledge of the sport. Articles also on other water sports, up to 3,500 words. Personal stories not wanted. PO Box 3473, Cape Town 8000, South Africa.

Thandi
This monthly specially for black Africans accepts submissions from overseas and is looking for success stories, general interest pieces, instructional items etc. Good quality photographs wanted. Payment negotiable. PO Box 2595, Johannesburg 2000, South Africa.

Spain
(Spanish Embassy, 39 Chesham Place, London SW1X 8QA)
With Spain's thriving tourist industry attracting large numbers of English-speaking visitors, some two dozen magazines are published regularly in English as well as several hundreds in Spanish. Virtually all the English language periodicals welcome freelance submissions. I once found a copy of one on a seat in a Madrid park and contributed to it regularly for the next three years. It is worth remembering more than 50,000 Britons live in Spain, most of them over retirement age. What do such folk want to read about? How to settle in a new country in their later years, the best ways of investing money, where and how to buy property, explanations of local and national customs, reassurance that all is well back home ... the list presents potential writers for Spanish magazines with plenty of choice.

Anyone who has ever been to Spain knows life seldom proceeds quickly and the Spanish Post Office is often a law unto itself. This is part of Spain's charm but it can protract editorial queries and replies over months or even years so be sure to extend lead times when wanting to sell copy for a dated future edition.

Andalucia Golf International
A monthly sports magazine sometimes featuring sports other than golf. Calvario 8, Edificio Marbelsun1, 2a 10, 29600 Marbella, Malaga, Spain.

Guidepost
Spain's weekly for Americans. Edificio Espana, Grupo 2, Piso 5, 28003 Madrid, Spain.

In Spain Magazine
A well-established monthly periodical. Calle Luna 4, 28120 Algete, Madrid, Spain.

Lookout
The monthly magazine of southern Spain, written in English. Pueblo Lucia, Fuengirola, Malaga 29640.

Speak Up
A monthly title for young adults learning to speak English. Generally welcomes lively but carefully-written articles about modern and current topics. Perez Galdos 36 bis., 185-1, 08021 Barcelona, Spain.

Swaziland
(Kingdom of Swaziland High Commission, 20 Buckingham Gate, London SW1E 6LB)

The Royal Flyer
The official magazine of Royal Swazi Airways. Bi-monthly and free, it is interested in receiving articles and pictures of quality on destinations around the world. Items on international cookery or shopping also welcome, up to 3,000 words. Jumbo Publications, PO Box A225, Swazi Place, Mbabane, Swaziland.

Sweden
(Swedish Embassy, 11 Montagu Place, London W1H 2AL)
Europa-Press (Saltmatargatan 8, 1st floor, Box 6410, S 113 82, Stockholm, Sweden) is a syndication agency wanting high quality features of international appeal on a wide variety of subjects for magazines in Sweden. Photographs also welcomed.

Scanorama
In-flight magazine, written in English, of Scandinavian Air Services. SAS, Media Partner, Galvegaten 18B, 113 30 Stockholm, Sweden.0

USA
(United States Embassy, 24 Grosvenor Square, London W1A 1AE)
'The state of journalism in the US at the moment is a polluted stream of tabloid lunacy, without honor, and produced by culturally illiterate incompetents who need a spell-checker to get the word "dog" correct.' So said author Harlan Ellison at the 1995

American Booksellers Convention – and such a comment does nothing to encourage magazine writers. This notwithstanding, the United States is the first market that comes to most writers' minds when they think of selling overseas and for the majority it is the best international marketplace.

There are a number of useful and interesting organisations writers might contact to their advantage, among them:

1 Council of Literary Magazines & Presses, 154 Christopher Street, Suite 3C, New York, NY 10014, USA.

2 Society of Professional Journalists, 16 S. Jackson, Greencastle, IN 46135-0077, USA.

3 Writers Alliance, 12 Skylark Lane, Stoney Brook, NY 11790, USA.

4 National Writers Association, 1450 S. Havana, Suite 424, Aurora, CO 80012, USA.

5 American Society of Journalists & Authors, Inc., 1501 Broadway, Suite 302, New York, NY 10036, USA.

6 Society of American Travel Writers, 4101 Lake Boone Trail, Suite 201, Raleigh, NC 27607, USA.

7 The International Women's Writing Guild, Box 810, Gracie Station, New York, NY, USA.

If you take writing seriously you need the two most authoritative American market guides published for potential contributors. Both are available from British bookshops or may be ordered directly. They are:

1 *Writer's Market*, Hi Marketing, Publishers' Sales & Marketing Agency, 38 Carver Road, London SE24 9LT. Tel: 0171 738 7751.
With some 800 new listings added to those updated from the previous edition, this massive tome details over 4,000 publications covering fiction, drama and small items as well as non-fiction. It includes an enormous amount of information about rights, research, freelance business matters, alternative opportunities, photographs and slides, postage, querying editors and fees. A huge section on consumer magazines covering every conceivable topic provides information, usually in great detail, often with editorial quotes about precise requirements. Writer's Market is published by F & W Publications, 1507 Dana Avenue, Cincinnati, Ohio 45207, USA.

2 *The Writer's Handbook*, The Writer, Inc., 120 Boylston St, MA 02116-4615, USA.
This invaluable reference book embraces the names, addresses, type of material wanted, rates of pay – and much more – of over 3,000 markets ranging from general interest, regional and city publications, family, lifestyle, environment, religion, health, business, college, literary and little magazines. Also included are no fewer than 110 chapters by the world's most successful authors, editors and literary agents. Distinguished writers share their experiences and discuss what worked for them. The creative process, inspiration, persistence, reaching your reader and many more topics are fully explored and explained.

So great are the opportunities for freelances in selling to American magazines it is sometimes difficult to sort out exactly what both you and they are looking for. If you want to write about retirement, for instance, an appropriate title could fall in the 'consumer' sector or, perhaps, in the huge 'women's' range. Always try to define the type of market before finding an individual title – and remember the less obvious markets are often those offering the best chances and many editors like material from writers new to them, giving the pages of their magazines a fresh 'voice'.

British Car
Bi-monthly covering British cars: historical/nostalgic, humour, interviews, people who buy them, collect them, drive them and love them. Half freelance material, written by and for enthusiasts. Photos with captions to accompany submissions. Sample copy and writers' guidelines available. PO Box 9099, Canoga Park, CA 91309, USA.

Cat Fancy
Monthly title 80-90% freelance-written for readers of all ages interested in every aspect of cats and cat-ownership. Writers' guidelines available. Fancy Publications Inc., Box 6050, Mission Viejo, CA 92690, USA.

Dragon Magazine
Ninety per cent freelance-written bi-monthly magazine of fantasy and science-fiction role-playing games. Very specialised: no general pieces required. 'A title,' says the editor, 'not understood by the average reader.' Study of past editions reveals contributors must be readers and share a serious interest in

gaming. Writers' guidelines available. TSR Inc., 201 Sheridan Springs, Lake Geneva, WI, USA.

Early American Life
Bi-monthly for 'people who are interested in capturing the warmth and beauty of the 1600 to 1840 period and using it in their homes and lives today. They are interested in arts, crafts, travel, restoration and collecting.' Looking for stories about real people doing something great to their homes and for good copy on any suitable topic. Length 750 to 3,000 words. Photos welcome. Buys first North American rights and accepts previously published articles. Sample edition and writers' guidelines available. Cowles Magazines, Inc., PO Box 8200, Harrisburg, PA 17105-8200, USA.

Interrace Magazine
Bi-monthly, 70% freelance-written, covering all aspects of inter-racial couples and families: folk who are of mixed parentage. Articles, general interest, humour, inspirational, historical/ nostalgic, interviews, opinions and personal experiences – all wanted. Sample edition and writers' guidelines available. Interrace Publications, PO Box 12048, Atlanta, GA 30355, USA.

Married Woman
For women in their twenties and thirties who have been married for ten years or less. Type of articles includes 'what to do about old boyfriends', 'coping with mother-in-law', 'managing money' etc – but be original. Send synopsis and clips of previous work. 1211 Avenue of the Americas, 2nd floor, New York, NY 10036, USA.

Online
Described as the 'Magazine of Online Information Systems' this bi-monthly is 95% freelance-written. Its readers are information professionals – librarians, authors or specialists in a wide range of subjects: people who regularly use online and Internet services. Its style is wholly practical, emphasising 'how-to' hints and techniques, and new products. Personal and technical experiences, and reviews of software and hardware are also featured. Knowledgeable writers only, please. PO Box 17507, Fort Mitchell, KY 41017, USA. (*e-mail*: ngarman@well.sf.ca.us)

Star Service
Keen to work with writers planning trips that would allow time for hotel reporting or living in major ports for cruise ships. Initial

queries should include details on writers' experience in travel and writing, cuttings, specific forthcoming travel plans and how much time would be available for hotel or ship inspection. Seeking objective and critical evaluation of hotels and cruise ships suitable for international travellers, based on personal inspections. Expertise in research and observation are essential: travel and travel-writing experience highly desirable. Writers' guidelines available. Reed Travel Group, 500 Plaza Drive, Secaucus, NJ 07096-3602, USA.

Zimbabwe
(High Commission of the Republic of Zimbabwe, Zimbabwe House, 429 Strand, London WC2R 0SA)

Everyhome
Dynamic home-orientated magazine not afraid to tackle frank and unrestricted issues for women going places in business – about being a parent, health, beauty, children etc. PO Box A680, Avondale, Harare, Zimbabwe.

Sportlight
Wants copy from overseas writers on sports and historical stories about sports. University of Zimbabwe, Sports Pavilion, MP 167, Mont Pleasant, Harare, Zimbabwe.

The Zimbabwe Fisherman
The country's leading angling publication. Open to factual copy and new ideas. Mag-set Publications Ltd, PO Box 6204, Harare, Zimbabwe.

The world ...
Japan, Taiwan, Korea, China, Singapore, the Philippines, Malaysia ... what we think of as the Far East stretches a long way and encompasses many very different lands. That means, in a writer's terms, many different readers. And what about the rest of the world? Wherever people live and read there will be markets for writers.

How far will your words reach round the globe?

8
Interviewing

Of all the tasks magazine journalists can undertake there is one that offers special pleasure: interviewing. For writers keenly interested in their fellow men (and women) what could be more fascinating than to sit down and talk to the famous, undisturbed by other folk, to ask whatever questions you like, to have the chance to observe your subjects' responses at close hand, to hear personal revelations and witness private emotional reactions – and to get paid for doing it?

We are not the only ones interested in others. People intrigue magazine readers. A survey of the contents of 100 magazines of various types including women's, general, hobby, entertainment and trade magazines shows more than 75% of editorial space features the lives, occupations, work and individual accounts of people with stories to tell. That last point is crucial in the business of interviewing – which is not the same as writing *about* someone. The latter is often called a 'profile' and may have a valid place in a magazine but an interview is as 'live' as any written piece on a page can be. An interviewer's job is to make readers feel they have met and talked with the interviewee.

Observation of the art of the live interview leads me to believe top-rate interviewers are born with some natural ability. But experts, and they are few in number, agree the craft can be learned and polished. This is particularly the case when considering written interviews which prove so popular with magazine readers.

The technique of interviewing, like all other forms of writing, follows a coherent pattern: an idea, research, preparation, the job itself and the write-up, perhaps with pix. Near the beginning of this sequence comes the most important part of the whole task, selling the interview. All these points are considered in this chapter, together with the one frequently worrying newcomers when they remember they only have one crack at the interview: can I do a good job?

Some folk are born with a greater depth of sympathy than others. John may by nature be more perceptive than Jack, Jean shrewder than Jane, Anne more experienced in life than Tom. Wherever you fit into such a pattern of human faculties and frailties, acquiring a good interview technique involves building on your abilities and strengthening your weaknesses. A good interviewer feels comfortable at the interview, relaxed (or giving the semblance of being relaxed) and able to make the interviewee feel at ease. Without apparent effort the interviewer sets the tone of that special one-to-one relationship that is apparent the minute we meet anyone for the first time: will we get on well together? He (I say 'he' with 'she' also in mind, of course) will conduct the interview with genuine pleasure even if it is just a job of work to be done. You may note I have mentioned the *semblance of being relaxed* and *without apparent effort*; although not every interviewer can summon tranquil feelings to order and first-time nerves persist in vexing us all, I have found the determined disregarding of such unwelcome emotions sends them packing with great speed as soon as the interview begins. Then it is conducted with genuine pleasure. So if you fear you lack the courage to interview anyone, let alone those well-known people magazine readers want to know about, take heart. Forget timidity and all will be well. Remember, too, neither the readers nor the interviewee need know about any private misgivings you may have any more than they are aware of the secret weapons you have already put to good use long before the interview takes place. For an interview needs careful and thorough preparation which is absorbing in itself.

The purpose of the interview

Before you begin it is wise to be honest with yourself about the purpose of conducting the interview you have in mind. Is it because the interviewee happens to live in your town? To satisfy your long-held hankering to talk to your favourite pop-star? Your kid brother would love a signed photograph of a First Division footballer? You might get a free trip to Spain to interview a leading film star? None of these reasons is adequate. There is only one valid question to ask yourself: will readers be interested? If the unbiased answer to this question is 'yes' then ask yourself *why* they will be interested. Will what the interview reveals give them help with a personal problem, perhaps, or encourage them to keep going in a difficult situation? Will they learn something practical, gain confidence, experiment with a craft, be safer drivers or understand the previously inexplicable?

There are many reasons why readers like reading published interviews; provide yourself with the answer to 'why?' and you will have a strong indication of how to build the framework of the task ahead.

We never actually met ...

Readers generally assume an interview is the result of a live face-to-face meeting between the two people involved but sometimes it may only be possible to conduct it by mail, fax, telephone or with a mixture of them all. While some professional interviewers scorn non-personal interviews, claiming the published results clearly lack the sparkle of 'live' ones, there may be a place on some occasions, for some reasons, and in some magazines, for interviews where the participants never meet. Do not discount 'distant' interviewing, therefore, but be careful not to fall back on it too readily and remember that warning about the possible 'lack of sparkle' that may result. Aware of this you will understand that there can be something (almost) irreplaceable about talking to someone face-to-face which leaves 'distant' interviews out in the cold. Conversations by letter may reveal invaluable insights into their writers' characters and personalities in our literature but the essence of an interview is its immediacy: its impact for magazine readers is that they, not you, were talking to and meeting the interviewee. A 'real' meeting may be the only way you can get a direct quote, hear your interviewee's voice – and perhaps its undertones revealing what he didn't say – and feel his friendliness. If you never met him it will be harder to let readers share these emotions. Users of *e-mail*, the facility for sending messages from one computer-user to another via the telephone system, realise the dangers of not being able to see or hear correspondents, and adopt a simple graphical code to indicate when the sender is anxious the recipient should not take offence. For instance, the 'smiley' :-) if you turn it through 90 degrees is the universal 'I'm only joking' sign.

If your interviewee lives hundreds of miles away or in another country and there is no chance of you going to see him you may have no alternative but to do the job by mail or phone. For the former, a carefully-worded list of questions can produce the best results. (Be sure to include an adequately-stamped addressed envelope to make it easy for him to reply.) To interview him by telephone it is best to arrange, by post, the date and time of your call – to suit him, of course – and to have a questionnaire of your own prepared. On the few occasions when I've had to interview someone by phone I've found myself wandering from my prepared list of questions as the moment gives rise to more pertinent ones. As this is likely to happen to your advantage (and the interview's) make sure you record the phone conversation if you have your interviewee's permission to do so; and get his agreement to being recorded on the tape itself. Some folk are uneasy knowing your electronic device is recording everything they say and if your interviewee is one of these you'll have to rely on your own handwriting. With practice your note-taking ability will improve but be careful to make it legible at all times. Not being able to read your own writing is always galling. Interview notes you can't decipher are particularly frustrating and may negate the whole enterprise. You only have one chance to make them. With the sophistication of modern recording equipment 'old-fashioned' shorthand is becoming a lost skill but I can't over-emphasise its value. Tape-recorders have their uses, but they cannot replace shorthand in every situation.

The initial approach

So where is this potential interviewee waiting for you to come along and write his story to dazzle editors and set the magazine pages on fire? There is no room for on-spec or seizing-the-opportunity interviews in magazine work as the pace of production of even the most frequently-published allows time to make all necessary arrangements and complete the work preceding publication.

The necessary preamble to interviewing demands study and research as dedicated as for any other type of writing. Someone in the public eye now may not be worth reading about when the magazine you are writing for is published, so the first factor to bear in mind is topicality. Consider the time-schedules discussed elsewhere in this book and discard anyone who may not be 'in' in, say, two months' time. Even people able to survive for this length of time in the public eye may have exhausted their special cachet by the time your interview would be published.

An unknown person might have a personal story that would make ideal material. So may someone revealing an achievement of particular interest to readers of your targeted magazine. As writing for a market is merely giving readers what they want, the choice of a person to interview is simply giving readers the person they want. Fortunately for writers, the world is full of 'ordinary' people. Many of them are caught up in events so dramatic, so thrilling, so tragic, so inspiring, so unbelievable or in some way so unusual that finding interviewees is not hard. Even though you will not sound out those already well-interviewed elsewhere or only available a costly distance away or likely to scorn your approach (although you can't be sure ...) or known to demand a fee for allowing you access (never, under any circumstances, agree to pay an interviewee for the so-called 'privilege' of interviewing him) there are still more than enough folk to interview, each with a different story to tell and an individual experience of life.

Thinking of or discovering interviewees is itself an exciting spur to the job ahead. Choices made, and armed with a list of several people . . .

First sell your interview

In the sequence of events leading to the interview, when is the best time to talk to editors and sell the idea? This may depend on how well you know the editor you have in mind and how well he knows you. From your experience of him, his likes, dislikes and favoured way of working, only you can decide which comes first: querying the editor about an interview with Mr X, or suggesting the same thing to Mr X while not yet being able to promise him it will be published. The matter is likely to be resolved without trouble if your work is already known to the editor and he can rely on you not suggesting an interview with someone unsuitable. Your friendly editor could invite you to go ahead, probably without any obligation on his part but perhaps with encouraging noises. He will certainly tell you if the idea is a non-starter, and if that is the case there may be no poor reflection on you or your abilities. The editor may know, as you can't, that he or a rival editor already has an interview with Mr X in the pipeline or that Mr X has refused to be interviewed for his magazine in the past. Mr X may, unknown to you, be considered more trouble than he is worth, demanding apologies and causing endless correspondence and aggravation.

A helpful editor may offer you suggestions about interviewees he would like to feature in his pages, but regardless of who originates the idea, if he is confident you can do the job he is likely to offer you a commission, i.e. a definite 'Yes, go ahead.' There is one important point to remember here: even being given a commission (and it makes no difference whether it is in writing or merely verbal, although you may feel happier with the former)

even a 'definite commission' is subject to the editor's evaluation
of the finished article. If the work's not good enough, cries of 'But
you promised ...' will fall on deaf ears. (See Chapter 11: Business,
for the legal position on this point.)

Supposing you have no previous contact with your chosen
magazine and are going in 'cold'? In this case it is better to establish contact with your potential interviewee, albeit having to
explain to him that you do not at this stage know where or even
if you are going to sell the piece. While this is not the most flat-
tering approach (and one guaranteed to offend well-known
figures) it is most unlikely you will find a magazine editor
commissioning an interview conducted by someone whose work
is totally unknown to him. At best you might get a loose 'We
don't mind having a look but can't promise ... ' which is not an
entirely satisfactory basis for the whole enterprise.

Whatever your relationship or non-relationship with the
editor of your choice, the selling of the interview is important to
the job itself even if it exists only on your wish-list at the time.
When you can tell a potential interviewee you have a commission to interview him for XYZ magazine his response is likely to
be far more positive.

This point emphasises three aspects of interviewing:

1 editors only commission writers whose work they know they
   can rely on;

2 to get to the above stage may take many sales and a long time;

3 interviewing for magazines is not for complete beginners.

Opinions wanted

This type of writing job has one facet contrary to all you may
have learned so far about mixing opinion with statements of fact.
'Readers don't want your views!' we are constantly reminded in
the general course of article-writing – but readers do want to hear
the opinions of someone sufficiently fascinating to be interviewed for the pages of a magazine. The degree of opinion you
quote will depend on the interviewee in question, of course, so
you will have to judge how much of what he says is relevant to
the background of the interview, i.e. why he was worthy of an
interview in the first place, and how much readers will want to
hear. For example, the opinion of a local councillor talking about
forthcoming cuts in the town's bus service may persuade you to

devote a high proportion of the interview to his justification or rebuttal of the scheme, while an interview with a young mother taking her baby to Switzerland for a rare operation might carry more opinions from medical authorities and specialists than from the mother herself. If the idea that opinions are wanted in interviews is new to you remember one essential adjunct: the opinions must not be yours.

Where and when

There are other reasons why it may be auspicious to contact your potential interviewee before making definite arrangements either with him or an editor. He might decline unless you can show some evidence of having done some of your homework when you first approach him, it could be difficult for an interview to be fitted into his hectic life, or he may insist on talking to you only in particular circumstances you cannot meet without problems. It is worth remembering some folk will be deterred by the word 'interview' but might agree quite happily to 'talk' to you: choose you words carefully while making sure you don't make any promises (about privacy etc) you will not be able to keep.

If you haven't already approached your interviewee you will need his consent to the project. Initial contact is best by phone (to his secretary or agent, perhaps, if not directly to him) but if you feel safer with written confirmation of all arrangements be prepared for the 'fixing' process to take longer and remember the topicality or purpose of the interview may suffer from such delay. Sometimes less well-known interviewees want to help with research in their own interests and this may be of benefit to you as long as they understand you are under no obligation to feature any particular aspect of their work or lives.

Explain who you are, which magazine will be publishing your interview, or you hope will be publishing it if you have not yet reached any editorial agreement, why you want to talk to him, about what, and indicate that you will readily fit in with his plans concerning dates, times, the use of a tape-recorder, the length of the interview and anything else to suit him.

If he says 'No' you'll have to decide whether he will give in if you're more persistent, he's learned to be wary of magazine interviews or he truly does not want the publicity a published interview will provide. Many newspaper interviewers are ruthless, pursuing reluctant victims, heedless of their wishes or protests: the results are frequently a source of complaints against journalists and editors. Because the pace of magazines is gentler don't imagine the business is any less tough in the commercial sense: money has to be made, circulation has to be maintained and preferably increased, and readers have to be satisfied. But on the whole interviews in magazines are arranged, given and published to the satisfaction of everyone concerned.

Where and when should the interview take place? If you are in a position to choose remember an interview over a meal is seldom wise. Balancing plates, pens, notebooks, eating, drinking, asking questions and recording answers all at the same time is not easy. Nor is it always a good idea to meet at your interviewee's home, although agreeing to such an invitation could make him feel more at ease than he might be elsewhere. Suggesting a venue where the interview is unlikely to be disrupted by outside influences such as children, animals and general interruptions is more sensible; and could be the first test of your tact and discretion.

Preparation

In any published interview some of the questions put by the interviewer may be just what you would have liked to ask if you had been doing the job. They flow with the natural informality of spontaneous conversation, giving readers a warm impression of being there. Writers aren't fooled. Questions that appear impromptu have been carefully planned and are cunningly inserted at the most appropriate moments. Background details of the interviewee's life, for example, may be mentioned casually but have been checked scrupulously long before the interview takes place.

Preparing the ground is part of most non-fiction work; certainly no magazine interview could succeed without it. Only later, at the interview itself, will the time and effort devoted to your groundwork prove its value. And here's a bonus: groundwork is engrossing. The facts about a celebrity's childhood, the early problems an 'ordinary' person overcame with extraordinary braveness or the details of a potential interviewee's lifestyle and habits may prove so interesting you may fear conducting the interview itself will be a disappointment by comparison. Don't worry; you can be sure the more thoroughly the earlier work is done the more pleasant will be the interview that follows.

It is important to discover all you can about your interviewee so you don't waste time at the interview asking him questions you could well have found answers to before you met. You will have confidence when you meet him if you already know about his early life, his family, his career, what he does in his spare time, what his hobbies are – in fact anything and everything that might be relevant (and probably quite a lot that may not be). Not only will such prior knowledge help you, it will also please him to realise you have taken the trouble to do your homework before the interview. Nothing irks an interviewee more than being asked questions like 'Where were you born?' or 'What is the name of your company?'

How to find the facts (for any purpose) is discussed in the earlier chapter on Research and much of the basic background about well-known people will be found in general reference material. But there are other sources of information. Colleagues working in the same field or friends sharing your interviewee's hobbies may be able to give you help not published in any book. They may also smooth your path with, for example, any special vocabulary or knowledge you will need to be familiar with when taking to him.

This can be invaluable, as I've found several times when about to interview people whose way of life or work has been foreign to me. Visiting a bakery before interviewing a local master baker gave me an insight, if only a brief one, into how the work was done and helped me understand what the master baker was talking about at the time of the interview. On another occasion taking trollies of library books round the wards in a large hospital taught me something of the value patients attach to the work of voluntary helpers. When this aspect of welfare arose during a subsequent interview with the boss of the hospital management committee I was better equipped to deal with it than I might otherwise have been. Another time a short outline from a Paraguayan acquaintance about the current history of his country put me in the picture to interview a Paraguayan diplomat who had fled to England and to understand why he was seeking refuge here. I also learned the names and aims of the warring factions in the coup he and his family were escaping from. So never miss the chance to gain some idea of the words or phrases your interviewee is likely to use and you won't have to keep asking him to explain what he means – which can be an irritant and inevitably impedes the flow of the interview.

Material already published will be useful but check it carefully; what may have been pertinent then may not be so now. Press releases, if appropriate, soon age and become valueless, and beware of any published items you find that do not bear the date of publication; they are, I suspect, just waiting for the unwary to come along and use them. They frequently spell trouble.

Collect everything together. If you find in due course you have gathered more information than you need remember it is better to have too much than too little. Later, as your experience grows, you will become more selective in your research. However well-practised an interviewer you may become, taking pains to get the 'feel' of the interviewee before meeting him will help you judge the best way of using the material you've collected.

Your private guidelines

Shaping your material into order is not difficult if you've assembled plenty of notes but before you begin you might want to refresh your mind about the format favoured by your intended market in interviews already published. This, after all, is the most important aspect of an interviewer's job – to satisfy readers. That done, decide the rough shape you'd like the interview to take. At this stage flexibility is important; setting yourself and the interviewee a programme that subsequently proves too rigid, predictable or boring will almost certainly read as rigid, predictable or boring when you come to write it up. So establish your guidelines but be prepared to depart from them.

In my early days of interviewing I kept in mind a sight I watch from the window over my desk. My cat climbs his favourite tree, often in a wild rush that takes him higher up the trunk than he intends to go, and then ventures out onto a side branch. A little way along he turns round, returns to the trunk and starts off along another branch lower down. He ventures along many branches of the tree, always returning to the central trunk before setting off again. And here's what impresses me: even when he has explored all the branches he wants to visit and could quite easily jump from the lowest to the ground he goes back to the trunk to make his final descent. It is a perfect example of always returning to the central theme, the trunk, and of rounding off an interview, or any writing job, by making a neat exit appropriate to where you began. And he's only a cat! (I think he might be a reincarnated writer.)

An interview is not just a question-and-answer session. 'What would I like to know about him?' is a good question to ask yourself. You might plan your questions chronologically beginning with your interviewee's childhood and family life, continuing with how his career began, his problems, achievements and so on, according to what is suitable to his story. But interviews conducted this way often drag even if they get off the ground at all. Opening with a reader-grabbing sentence or question, like my cat's dramatic dash up the tree, is as important in interviewing as it is in any other type of writing. Available space may also preclude telling the subject's entire story. Your decision about where to start will be determined by what your market wants and, above all, whatever it is that makes your interviewee of special interest to readers at that time. Your thoughts on how to plan the questions to ask must be tempered by these considerations.

Just as some computer software programs aim to help you sort out the planning of any article, others are designed to ease the pattern of interview questions and answers. Despite this particular technological aid I generally begin with paper and pencil, writing down key questions as they occur to me on a large sheet of paper, leaving plenty of space between items so I have room for adding subsidiary questions. This way I can change my mind about where to start and what to ask at any particular point in the interview. There is often a great deal of reorganizing and inserting new ideas before I am temporarily satisfied with my outline plan.

It is wise to keep opening questions of a general rather than a specific nature and not to plunge into anything likely to be controversial or provoke your interviewee to apprehension or hostility. Questions that vary in length and depth are most easily answered but avoid those requiring only a 'yes' or 'no' response. Indicate your genuine interest with thoughtful and sympathetic questioning and your interviewee will be encouraged to expand on his replies with greater relaxation and warmth, speaking more freely and informally. Ideally, to the innocent reader, an interview should seem to be a spontaneous conversation.

You may find, perhaps to your surprise, that you have a formidable amount of information about your interviewee, especially if he is well known. How can you handle all these notes during the interview? This is when you must choose which aspects of his life or work can you skate over or leave out altogether. Maybe he is a fine amateur cook or a keen rock-climber: if you are interviewing him for, let us say, his fame as a brilliant tenor you may decide not to refer to either the cooking or rock-climbing. But dropping such intriguing snippets into the conversation can lend it extra interest so you might bear these other activities in the back of your mind (with single word reminders in your guidelines such as 'cook' or 'rocks'), ready to bring them to the fore if the moment seems propitious.

Preparing the notes I'm going to take with me, I leave plenty of space after each question for the interviewee's reply if I'm relying on my own shorthand or notes. A second sheet behind the first will carry subsidiary questions and reminders of anything I might forget as well as quick *aides-mémoire* to the basic statistics about my interviewee. Even if this back-up sheet is not consulted or glanced at again, merely knowing it is there is a great boost to my confidence. If you plan to use a portable recorder make sure it is reliable and that you are very familiar with how it works. There are several good models available, not all are expensive or difficult to operate and using one will free you from having to take your eyes from your interviewee and his surroundings.

Face to face

Remember to take everything you're going to need for the interview (including your watch) and arrive promptly; for an interviewer who wants to set a cool, calm and collected scene that means get to the appointed place before the arranged time. Bring your equipment out casually during friendly talk before the interview begins. You may also like to confirm how long he expects it to last. Do you feel more comfortable with your watch on the table or on your wrist? Checking the time too obviously may be annoying for both of you. Also consider whether you want your notebook on your lap or on a table. It's on my lap almost every time so I can hold it up if I like and don't have to lift and lower my head to consult and take notes (I can also keep him in the corner of my eye when he thinks I'm not looking at him). Maintaining good eye contact with your interviewee is likely to make the conversation flow smoothly and there will be less jerkiness between your questions and his answers.

If daylight is likely to fade before the interview is over will you still be able to see him and your notes? Will he be able to hear you distinctly (might he be a little deaf?) and will you hear his answers clearly? How much small talk should you indulge in at your meeting? It's natural to be a little nervous, particularly if you've never met your interviewees before; some interviewers, like some actors, claim it keeps the adrenaline flowing and is more of a help than a hindrance. Your man (or woman) may have more interview experience than you have and may even take advantage of your nervousness. Or it could be that he has never been interviewed before and is more apprehensive than you are;

this may lead to him trying to pretend, quite involuntarily, that he has had a good deal of experience in dealing with folk like you. Don't worry. If he seems truculent or semi-hostile in your first moments together be careful not to react in the same manner. You are not meeting him as a 'friend', although ideally your interview will be on friendly terms and you may emerge from it with a real liking for him, but as a job. This may sound cold and calculating but it must be foremost in your mind: you want something out of him. Happily there is often a softening of any opening danger signals as the interview progresses and you both get into your stride. I recall several instances where my first feelings proved wholly mistaken and can truly say I have never conducted a magazine interview I have not thoroughly enjoyed. These points about lighting, hearing and initial impressions are generally resolved instinctively without any trouble when you settle down. Now it's time to begin ...

After the first few moments you will find you've forgotten any initial nervousness; this is the time for concentration. As you ask your questions and take note of his replies (if you are not recording them) don't be so keen to have your next question ready that you don't really listen to what he's saying. Even with a recorder, you are taking part in a two-way conversation and how that goes will determine the way in which you ask your questions. Your attitude will affect the interview and his may be particularly revealing. Crossing the knees towards another person is, I'm told by experts, a sign of being at ease with him. Does your interview feel at ease with you? If you're inserting questions you've only thought of when the interview is in full swing, so much the better. And don't be afraid of acknowledging a mistake if you make one: such sincerity will elicit greater relaxation and more spontaneous replies to your questions.

Maintaining the tone of the interview is all important. Needle your interviewee and he may stay silent. Irritate him and you could be shown the door. If you have established a certain rapport you may be able to ask a 'risky' question, perhaps as if you've only just thought of it, that might give you some of your most valuable information. With a light touch, an understanding attitude and sympathetic assessment of his preferred pace, there is a time to keep silent in most interviews. The whole purpose, after all, is to get him to do the talking and the fewer questions you have to ask the better. Just a nod or an understanding smile may be appropriate at times and a little break may be useful for both of you. While he or somebody else organises a cup of tea you will be catching up on your next question and any notes you've taken so far.

Oh . . .

Interviewing is a satisfying job but just occasionally it can go wrong. If you have prepared the ground thoroughly this is not a frequent occurrence, but the most likely problem could concern what your interviewee does or does not want you to write – accompanied by coercion, bribes, warnings or even threats. Fortunately such rare occasions are easy to deal with; you simply walk out as politely as you can in the circumstances. You will, of course, have to tell your editor you cannot proceed and there will be no published interview.

Interviewing is immensely enjoyable and often surprising. You may think you have it all resolved and that everything has gone as you planned it would and then – wham! He drops a bombshell: he's left his wife, he's emigrating or whatever, in his context, is dramatic news. When that happens you have a news break that can't wait for an interview in a magazine to be printed a few weeks or even months hence. You have an item for a newspaper – but that's another story.

Writing it up

I advise writing it up as soon as you can, thereby lessening the risk of thinking something was said when it wasn't. It's wise to set down on paper as soon as you possibly can any specially valuable parting comments he made that you couldn't record and have been nurturing in your head all the way home. If you've done your market study well you know you have to catch your readers' attention at the very start.

Your task is to make them feel they had been talking to your interviewee, not you. Perhaps he said something that made you laugh? Did anything give you a jolt or intrigue you? If it did, it will do the same for readers. Once launched on the job of writing it up you can deftly set the scene of where the interview took place to help readers picture it. They want to know about people, with only enough background of their houses and families to help establish an image so don't labour the point. It is better to drop such information in gradually and almost casually so it may be absorbed by readers without them being aware of what they are taking in.

The less of 'you' in the interview the better and your market will indicate just how you appear at all. As a friend telling readers how you went to interview Mr X and what you found? Or does your editor favour an unadorned Question and Answer format? Are you writing your questions in direct speech ('What has given you the most pleasure in life?') or reported speech ('I asked what had given him the most pleasure in life')? The former brings interviews alive but a balance of the two gives them a natural feeling. Only you can judge the best tone for your written interview but guard against flippancy even if your interviewee and the purpose of the interview are in the 'joky and fun' category. Toss it off too lightly, with the best of intentions, and you may lose your readers' confidence.

Filing

The task is finished. 'Filing', in professional jargon, simply means sending or taking it to your chosen magazine. But wait: there may still be one or two points to attend to.

Don't forget to enclose any pictures you might have offered the editor to go with your interview and a stamped self-addressed envelope unless you are certain he won't feel a pang of irritation when he doesn't find one. After so much work and effort on your part it would be a shame to risk spoiling your chances for the sake of a postage stamp.

One thing leads to another ...

When your interview is published there is one further minor job to be done. Send a copy of the magazine carrying it to your interviewee, even though you think he may have seen it already, with a brief 'Thank you' note. He'll be pleased at this small courtesy but there is more than politeness behind this simple gesture. If his friends or working colleagues are equally good interview material you may find one working assignment you thoroughly enjoyed can lead to another ...

9
Presentation

If you like everything neat and tidy when the job is finished the task of presenting it to your chosen editor can be pleasantly satisfying. The writing's completed, everything's in good shape and all that remains is to send off your copy. You will know the person to send it to and the correct address if you've dealt with the editor or features editor. But if you've only spoken to a voice on the phone at the preliminary stages (which may have been quite a while ago) or, worse still, are submitting to a magazine out of the blue, you may be unsure about how it should be addressed. Do you send an accompanying letter, and if so, what should it say? Can you ask the magazine's office to telephone you to confirm your work has arrived safely? Should you send more than one copy? How big should be the stamped self-addressed envelope you send with your copy or does sending one at all tell the recipient you are expecting it to be rejected? These and similar questions beset newcomers to writing for magazines. But the matter of presentation is, in fact, both simple and painless.

Office organisation

Knowing how a magazine is organised and how its office is run (or should be run, which is not always the same thing) is helpful. Just as efficient organisation in your kitchen at home differs from that necessary for the smooth running of the kitchens behind the scenes at a large international restaurant, so magazine offices differ in the way they are arranged and managed.

The size of the staff, the space in the office, the age, capability and effectiveness of its equipment and the overall confidence of the whole setup is ruthlessly determined by one thing: profitability. New readers must be attracted and old ones retained; everything must be done for the maximum impact, often with a depleted staff and an increasingly restricted budget. How is it done?

Magazines of substantial size and those running as part of large groups are generally organised into five main departments:

1 editorial – which is what mostly concerns writers;

2 advertising – persuading clients to buy magazine space in which to advertise their wares;

3 production – printing and handling the physical making of the magazine;

4 sales – dealing with circulation and distribution;

5 administration – running the office, perhaps the building as well, the secretarial side, finance, stationery, insurance and everything else that needs attending to.

All five departments cost money to run but only two, advertising and sales, produce income. In times of financial stringency even the money raised from cover prices may barely compensate for the costs of running the sales department. That leaves advertising as the only positive source of income and no consumer magazine can last long in that unhappy situation.

There is a great deal of contact between the various departments, the more so in a small setup where a handful of staff may do almost everything. As for the production: most magazines are printed by contract printers who may be located in a town miles from the office, in a different part of the country or even overseas.

Who does what

Back to the editorial side. If you have made contact with the editor (or the features editor if that is the appropriate person to deal with for the magazine you are targeting) you have already passed the first hurdle and if your work has been definitely commissioned it will not be subject to a further decision at this stage.

But if you are going in 'cold' the first person likely to read your work will be the copy-taster. On smaller publications this may well be the assistant editor. He (and of course that also means 'she' as throughout this book) will make a quick assessment as to whether it is worth passing to the editor or features editor. The editor himself may be the person who reads unsolicited scripts if staff numbers are low and that is how he prefers to handle the office management. A favourable decision – and you've moved up one important step.

A copy-taster is an experienced staff journalist who knows the requirements of the magazine like his own back garden and can quickly recognise what is or could be made acceptable. When faced with a pile of unsolicited copy anyone making the decision about what to accept is likely to take only what is absolutely right for the magazine and throw the rest out. When something is so good it can't be ignored, why bother with other material that needs cutting or rewriting? So make sure the copy that simply can't be put down is *yours*.

The editor of a magazine is the absolute arbiter of what is or is not printed on its pages and is closely involved in everything that goes on until an edition is complete and ready to hand to the printers. Some of the best editors care for their magazines as a parent loves a child: wanting it to be superior to its rivals, anxious for everyone to love it more than any other and agonizing when something in its life turns out badly. Being an editor is hard work demanding much practical experience but having a love for the job undoubtedly pays dividends. If you meet an editor who declines to discuss amendments or improvements about what you offer, remember that the interests and needs of the magazine are his priorities.

If the magazine has a large number on the staff you may be dealt with by the features editor without direct reference to the editor. There will be consultation in editorial meetings about the contents of a particular issue where your work will be published, but be assured there is official approval from the editor for whatever the features editor may tell you.

Only a carefully-determined proportion of magazine space is reserved for features. Revenue-earning advertisements take precedence although some magazines in the non-commercial category don't take any. Features compete with editorial matter (that sometimes means little chats by the editor or announcements of what's coming in future issues), fiction (if any), reviews, regular columns and whatever else will appeal to readers. Pictures of all sorts, including those accompanying features, are usually dealt with separately (see the next chapter).

How can you best fit into the daily working plan of a magazine office? Giving a good impression with well-presented work is important. Make it easy to handle as soon as it is opened. Don't include a mixed bag such as a letter, some pictures, a caption sheet, a list of suggested ideas for the editor to consider in the future, a stamped self-addressed envelope, a yes/no questionnaire to be completed and returned and –

horror of horrors – more than one article crammed in a single package. Yes, there are such unappetising submissions regularly received in magazine offices and unless the person with the task of sorting them out is feeling exceptionally well-disposed to humanity they will be returned unread if they don't end up in the wastepaper basket.

But if your submitted copy is properly presented you can be sure it will be happily received, particularly by magazines which genuinely want your envelope to contain just what they are looking for. Once past the acceptance test it will be closely scrutinised by a sub-editor whose job is to make all freelance and staff-written copy ready to be printed.

The first task for the sub-editor is to fit your copy into the space on the page or pages allotted by the chief sub-editor. Then the sub (as sub-editors are commonly called) will correct grammar and punctuation to conform to the house style. He will also write crossheads (those mini headlines that help break up long articles and make them easier to read) and retitle the copy if he thinks it necessary. Don't take offence if the heading you gave the article is discarded: a new one may be chosen simply because yours contained more words than would fit in the allotted space or because, unknown to you, an adjacent headline clashes with your original title.

Please note that few magazines see it as their job to check your facts and figures. Sub-editors are too busy preparing information for the printers: the size, shape and typeface required for each story, the page numbers, order, column width and everything else keep them fully occupied. So the more you can do to ease their work the happier they will be. A sub needs a sound knowledge of the laws of libel and contempt for fear the magazine gets into trouble. He knows, and writers should remember, that libel is 'a published false statement, false accusation or malicious falsehood or misrepresentation in print, damaging to a person's reputation.' A sub is also very familiar with all the other work involved in every stage of publication and, of course, of the magazine's edition deadlines. He must see all copy is in good taste, good English, of the required length and shape while within the aim of the writer and the needs of the reader. I'm inclined to agree with fellow journalists who claim sub-editors, and particularly chief subs, are the most important people on the staff of magazines.

Most professional = least trouble

The whole aim of submitting to a magazine is to please the readers and that means pleasing the editor. By chance I once discovered the editor of a local weekly magazine was a keen golfer (a sport about which I know nothing) so I sent him a piece about the early life of a well-known player who had spent his formative years in the area. Good luck? Yes, but more a case of taking advantage of it. You can do the same. Has the editor you're aiming at a published record of earlier posts held in the magazine or newspaper world? Has he any particular likes or dislikes? He'll certainly have the interests of his magazine at heart, as we've said above, and when he sees copy about something that particularly appeals to him he may find himself instinctively softening ...

Close study of the market reveals what an editor likes but keep your eyes and ears open for sudden editorial changes. Editor A might favour the type of story you have been at pains to research and write but before you have time to submit it he has gone and editor B has taken over. What do you do? First of all find out whether editor B is of the same mind as his predecessor. He is unlikely to be so because the fact that the old editor was (perhaps) sacked indicates the magazine management was not happy about the way he was running it. Up to a point the new man will have to keep within the confines of established editorial policy, particularly if the magazine is part of a large publishing house, but new brooms can seldom resist sweeping clean.

If you are unsuccessful with editor B discover where editor A has gone. I've found the best way to do this is the simplest: ring up the office and ask whoever answers on the switchboard. If editor A has taken over another magazine which is at all suitable for what you have written and you're prepared to make whatever alterations are necessary you could be back in business after all.

Helping yourself

If you've read of writers submitting hand-written work to editors with passages crossed out, crude insertions at the side of the text and arrows pointing to intended positions of whole paragraphs, allow yourself a fond smile but *don't do the same*. Such practices may have been acceptable years ago but are certainly not so now. Knowing how to type is an invaluable bonus for writers. Learning to type has proved its worth to me many times over: typing is fast and easy at the rough draft stage of writing copy and with the simple editing facilities offered by a good word-processor final copy can be produced at speed. Best of all, with the eyes not on the keyboard a touch typist can edit work on the screen without effort and that is also a time saver. If you use a word-processor but cannot yet type well, why not try one of the software programs designed to teach you touch-typing? It may require patience to learn but you'll always be glad you did.

Here are a few extra tips to help you give editors what they want in the way they want it:

1 Don't use the word 'page' when identifying sheets of paper on which your copy is written. To magazine staff the word 'page' refers to the page of the magazine as it will eventually be printed. So anything bearing the legend 'page 2', for instance, refers to page 2 of the magazine. If a sheet of your copy becomes detached and is found with 'page 2' at the top it may be assumed to be copy marked up to appear on page 2 of the edition being prepared at the time – which may not be what the editor has in mind at all. To be sure your work doesn't suffer in such confusion always mark sheets of your copy with the word 'folio', i.e. 'folio 2' not 'page 2'.

2 Discover the width of a publication's standard typesetting and make your copy observe the same width. If you both work in 9pt Garamond over 15 picas, for instance, making about 45 characters per line, the space your copy will need is quickly and easily estimated – endearing you to the editorial staff.

3 Send two copies of your article. The second should be clearly marked DUPLICATE on every folio so it causes no bewilderment. It will be plainly seen to be a duplicate copy if you print it on coloured paper. It may never be used or referred to but could be invaluable if any queries arise.

4 Don't send more than one item of copy in a single envelope.

5 Don't supply a stamped-address envelope large enough for your copy's return, particularly if it is short; enclose a letter-size envelope instead. Finding a ready-to-return envelope in his hand may tempt a busy editor to stuff your copy in it and wing it back to you without further thought. But if your work is left lying around the office it may be picked up again at some less fraught time and receive more considered (and favourable) treatment.

Why do you want it back, anyway? If you have to submit it elsewhere it will be better to present a new clean copy to another
market.

Personal stationery

You've finished editing your article and reach for your first sheet
of top-copy paper. If you have headed paper printed on A4 giving
your name, address and other details, do not be tempted to use it
for the first folio of your copy. Headed paper is important for
letters and conveys an impression of you as a writer even before
you've printed a word on it. What it says and how the information
is laid out gives anyone seeing it an immediate concept of you,
your likely attitude to work and your probable capability.

Let your headed paper state your name clearly in not-too-
fancy a typeface without a title (Mr, Mrs etc) but with any professional or academic qualifications you may possess. Your address,
telephone, fax number and e-mail address are the only other
important requirements, but don't worry if you do not have the
last two. I know writers who also display as part of their credentials a list of magazines they have contributed to; I don't do this
for fear a fixed list would be not be suitable for every letter I
might want to write when submitting to a variety of editors in
widely different markets – but it is a matter of personal choice.
Desktop publishing programs on home computers and facilities
in local copy-shops make the inclusion of little pictures (known
as 'clip art') simple and appealing and it is all too easy to make
your name look hand-written or decorate your headed paper
with logos and monograms and fancy bits. Overindulgence can
be a mistake: giving a bright and businesslike impression does
not depend on gimmicks although a plain modern logo editors
come to associate with a particular writer may be a help.

The same basic design can be used for paper of different sizes
like A5 (half the size of A4, either way up), compliments slips and
business cards. Even small sticky labels can carry a part of your
overall design to keep everything looking like *you*.

A pleasure to read

Copy sent to an editor should be clean, uncluttered and easy to
read. That means using white A4 paper (21mm wide by 29.5mm
deep) of at least 70 grams in weight, and preferably 80 grams. If
you can discover any special likes or dislikes the editor of your

intended market has about receiving copy you'll be in luck. The frequently-quoted recommendation to freelances that the first sheet should indicate only the sender's details with the article's title, wordage and available rights, leaving the article proper to start on the second sheet is no longer appropriate in most editorial offices where such offerings instantly tell the staff that the writer is an amateur. Of course there is nothing wrong in being an amateur (who didn't start that way?) but to labour the point is tantamount to saying 'Please give me special consideration because I'm only a beginner.' And in a busy and commercially-orientated magazine office that can be the kiss of death.

It is neater, more sensible and generally acceptable to begin your article on folio one with what is known as a 'catch-line' at the top indicating everything the editor, the copy-taster and anyone else needs to know. Like this:

Jill Dick / *Our Cats* / for Martin Wilkes / purring (1200) 1 of 5

This catch-line is not underlined but is followed by two blank lines to keep it distinct from the copy itself. It indicates:

1 Who the copy is from – in this case, me – with what is known as a 'by-line'.

2 The title of the magazine – *Our Cats* (in case more than one magazine is dealt with in the same office).

3 The intended recipient – features editor Martin Wilkes.

4 The article is about purring, is 1200 words long, and this is the first of its five folios.

Subsequent sheets carry the same catch-line with folio numbers altered as required. A 'tag' to identify the article, like 'purring' in the example above, should befit its substance but be original and don't use 'Christmas' during the festive season when many other pieces besides yours may have the same tag.

So forget that old-hat 'cover-sheet'. Of course it is important to state all relevant information about your copy somewhere but what doesn't appear on your catch-line is better specified in a short covering letter, if it hasn't already been discussed and settled in earlier correspondence.

All typing must be in double spacing on one side of the sheet only. There should be plenty of white space at the top and foot of each and on both the left and the right of typed text. I generally set my guidelines to leave a minimum 3cm space on the left, 4cm or 4.5cm at the top and 4cm at the foot.

The space on the right side of the sheet will vary unless the text is 'justified'. That means setting a fixed margin on the right and causing the letters and/or words on each line to spread themselves out to keep the right edge straight. It is done automatically for body text on the pages of books such as this which would look untidy without it. You will see, too, that every letter is 'proportional' here: the letter 'i', for example, is narrower in print than the letter 'w' and the four-letter word 'till' takes up less width than the four letters in 'maze'. Although modern technology makes proportional typing and justification a simple process editors usually prefer to receive straightforward unjustified text, claiming is quicker and easier to read. So when your typing machinery produces a right margin that is ragged (meaning not every line ends exactly under the one above) make sure there is a good white space some 3.5cm wide on the right-hand side.

Indent all paragraphs except the first by three or four spaces and write 'more' or 'mf' at the foot of each folio except the last which should end simply with the word 'end'. A word-processor makes it easy to write at, say, 64 characters (i.e. letters, spaces or punctuation marks) per line and 25 lines per sheet. If you are using a typewriter make a small pencil mark on the paper to remind you when you have typed the 25th line but remember to erase the pencil mark before sending your work out. You think 64 characters is too short a line and there could be more than 25 lines per sheet? This is matter of individual preference but having seen the space most sub-editors need for their instructions to typesetters, layout men etc, I like to give them plenty. It is important to close your copy with an accurate statement of its wordage. When the piece is published you may find an editor disagrees with the number of words you have quoted but this is because editors have to pay heed to the amount of space your copy will occupy on a page. There will be sub-heads, for example, inserted either by you or a staff sub-editor, so enough space must be reserved for these – and they will fill more space on the page in a larger font than that used for body text.

As for the type itself: whatever your choice of faces and fonts, use the plainest, clearest and neatest your machine can produce and if your printer or typewriter uses a ribbon check it is well-inked. Did you hear about the radio station presenter reading out a letter from a listener who said he was 111? There was a pause before the presenter continued. 'No, he's not 111. He's ill.' As ribbons get faint use them for rough drafts and letters to long-suffering friends but always keep a new or re-inked one (or a spare ink cartridge) in your store cupboard.

Punctuation has been referred to in an earlier chapter but don't be offended if you find your copy has undergone major surgery when it is eventually published. If ever we writers have high horses to get on it won't be until we are at least in the Graham Greene class. He submitted an essay to a leading Sunday newspaper which returned a proof revealing the insertion of a single comma for the sake of enhanced clarity. The famous writer responded immediately; unless the extra comma was removed he would not allow the piece to be published.

Paper talk

If you type or print an article, other than a very short one, from beginning to end without anything to lighten it (except the indents for new pars) the result can look uninviting, demanding conscious effort of concentration from readers: effort they may not bother to make. Even to an editor's eyes an unbroken slab of text is a burden and that's the last impression you want to give him. Duty tells him to read it and break it up if it's going to be of any value. If the writer can't see how dull and boring such unbroken presentation is, he might say to himself, the content of the article is probably just as dull and boring ...

There are several ways of making your copy look more appetising even though some may be ignored when the piece is published. Introducing new aspects of the subject matter with subheadings, for example, is effective in softening the text. Subheads are sometimes called 'crossovers' or 'breathers' for obvious reasons. Just as the article's title may be changed so may other aspects of presentation without any reflection on you. Only a sub-editor can know how and where your copy will sit on the page and only he will be in a position to retain, edit or delete your subheads or to insert others elsewhere in your copy if he thinks fit.

Boxes

Boxes come in a different category; you may hear them referred to as 'side-bars' which in essence are the same thing. Imagine you have written an article referring to statistics on, for example, the incidence of car theft in the UK over the past five years. To quote precise figures in the text would slow it up considerably, so it is preferable to put all the factual information together in a ruled box that will appear somewhere on the page beside or beneath the main body of your copy. This way readers can check statistics for themselves with all the information laid before them in one easily-assimilated block. There are many articles that benefit from an accompanying 'box' presentation although more than one or two per article may be over-egging the pudding and give your presentation a 'bitty' appearance. Boxes can hold any useful instruction or data or messages in a brief, crisp and easy-to-read format: lists of ingredients for recipes, for instance, names and addresses of organisations to contact, or a description of how to reach a particular venue named in the body text.

Attracting attention is another reason for using boxes, whatever they contain, and the first person to attract will be the editor. It is best to present a box on a sheet separate from the main article but firmly attached to it with a 'more' indication at the foot of the body text so the box is not overlooked. The word 'end', of course, will then be moved to the foot of the sheet carrying your box.

Bullets and come-ons

In magazine parlance 'bullets' are items of text marked with black blobs or special editorial symbols. Writers use them to draw attention to, for example, a list of objects. Generally it doesn't matter how you highlight such a list and you may prefer to number its items 1, 2, 3, 4, and so on. If your editor obviously likes special symbols (and your typewriter or word-processor can provide them) use them to liven up your presentation and give it variety.

A 'come-on' is just what its name suggests: an editorial device to tell readers it will be worth their while taking notice. A come-on will often be a sentence or a few phrases taken from the copy and repeated in bold type in a ruled or unruled box in the middle of the published article. Although writers do not actively decide which passages in their copy will make good come-ons (that is another job for the sub-editor), wise ones will try to provide plenty of tempting phrases just crying out to be used in this way.

Pins, staples and clips

If you want to annoy the folk dealing with your copy fasten the sheets together with pins to prick their fingers. To be truly beastly get busy with your stapler. That way you offer them the choice of hunting for one of those little gadgets sold specially for unstapling staples, wrecking the ends of paper knives and the like if they don't have the de-staplers to hand, or just pulling stapled sheets apart to leave torn corners – and perhaps torn pages.

Paperclips are cheap, have no sharp edges, come in plastic or metal, in plain or bright colours and offend nobody. I'm so fond of them I can't bear to part with unusual ones that come my way and one day hope to be the reigning champion (if sole member) of the Unusual Paperclip Society. Meanwhile I never risk spoiling a good impression (built with hard work and patience) by forgetting what appears trivial but may be important: only use paperclips to fasten sheets together.

Covering letters

Whether you are going in 'cold' or not and regardless of whether you are submitting a single sheet piece or a twenty-sheet article, enclose a brief covering letter. When you submit copy to a magazine it is assumed (without the need to say so directly) that you are offering it for sale, i.e. for financial reward.

Special care must be taken if you have not been in touch with the editor or anyone on his staff before submitting your contribution (although I would discourage this approach) when you will need to enclose a *brief* CV. I heard a young man explain to another that CV stood for 'Current Value': it is, of course, an abbreviation of *curriculum vitae*, Latin for 'a summary of life'; more precisely, it is a written summary of one's personal details and the main events of one's education and career, usually produced to accompany job applications – which, in effect, this is. Make sure your CV or first letter to the editor is informative but concise. Confine it to what he needs to know and remember you are trying to sell yourself as well as an idea – for unless you assure him you can do the job as he would like it done the idea will fall on stony ground. Mention any journalistic and other relevant qualifications and experience you have but forget your achievements in netball if you are writing a cookery piece, for instance. List published work – within reason. Think of what qualifies you to write the piece you are offering. If expert knowledge is important in the writing of your article, perhaps with the safety of readers in mind, for example, state if you can claim such expertise.

Do not refer to anything that needs a written reply which will tempt the editor to put the whole package to one side until he or his secretary has time to deal with it, thus losing the immediate impact you are striving for. Observe the following:

1 Address it to the correct person (if you don't know the name ring up and ask the switchboard).

2 Put your phone number on your letter, as unostentatiously as possible if it doesn't already appear on headed paper bearing your address.

3 Get to the point immediately after the Dear X salutation.

4 The point will be either: 'Please find enclosed XXX words on "Pearl diving in Japan" (or whatever) as agreed in our correspondence last month.'

Or 'Please find enclosed XXX words on "Pearl diving in Japan" which I hope you will find of interest.' In the latter case follow with another short par outlining your experience and/or knowledge for writing such a piece.

5 State what rights you are offering and the fee agreed, if any (see Chapter 11: Business).

6 State if any pix are enclosed (see Chapter 11: Pix).

7 Sign off.

Envelopes

Your copy is perfectly presented and you're ready to put it in the envelope – at last. If it is short enough to be carried on a single sheet folding it into three for a 22cm x 11cm envelope will suffice. For two or three sheets I recommend folding once to A5 size and inserting in an envelope of the same size. For copy of more than three sheets you should use an envelope large enough to take the entire pack without any folding. You must also be sure your envelope is adequately stamped. A postal weighing machine is a useful investment. When your package includes pix make sure they are sandwiched between stiff card or padding for protection.

Always enclose a stamped self-addressed envelope. Why should anyone reply if you don't? Stamps and envelopes cost money. Even if you have been in earlier contact with the editor or someone on his staff I advise sending a stamped self-addressed envelope: it is a mistake to presume on what might be a relationship less firm than you think it is, the person you dealt with before may have gone away and, in any case, politeness always pays.

Is the whole business of paper, envelopes and snail-mail out of date? Few magazine editors will yet accept contributions on disk, despite the advance of technology and computerisation in production departments. Whether to accept disks will be the decision of the production editor, and compatibility can be a difficulty. But if the answer is 'yes' submitting copy in PC or Macintosh format will generally be acceptable; but be sure to check with the magazine first. Remember you may not get the disk back and you will almost always have to submit 'hard' copy (on paper) as well – so there is more work to be done, not less. And for what? Disk submission may be the way in the future but until varying formats can also hold all known design and layout codes it is, at the time of writing, more likely to be a hindrance than a help.

Despatch

Whatever rules and tips you read or hear, remember this one: it is truly the most important of all:

NEVER PART WITH THE ONLY COPY OF YOUR WORK.

Terrible tales are told by unfortunate writers who have left the only copy of an article/short story/novel/radio play etc on a bus or a train, in a cafe or a shop. Some thieves and burglars even stoop as low as to ignore the family silver and make off with uncopied manuscripts, depriving the writer of what he treasures most and insurance companies can never replace. Unless you want to experience such a nightmare always make a copy of everything you write. It doesn't matter whether you use old carbon paper to provide a smudgy blue or black copy as you write or type, whether you frequent a traditional copy shop or whether you have the most sophisticated disk-copying method money can buy: only the security of having a copy (or more than one copy if this paragraph makes you nervous) safely tucked away in a separate place will allow you to sleep easily at night.

Don't wait until you lose your only copy. A mystic law decrees you will lose it if it's your only one. I don't know why if you have at least one backup, the law doesn't apply.

10
Pix

There is no doubt the majority of magazines would barely survive without illustrations. Dull slabs of prose can be decidedly unattractive, no matter how inventive sub-editors might be in trying to break them up and lighten their impact. Because illustrations are desperately needed and appropriately targeted articles with accompanying pix (as they are commonly called) often find good homes, offering editors a double package increases your chances of making regular sales at good rates.

It almost goes without saying that the photographs must be good; and 'good' in this sense means they are just what the editor wants and better than he could find for himself. The latter point is particularly worth noting, for why should he pay you unless your pix are better than those his own sources can provide? All consumer magazines have access to their own stocks of assorted pictures or can buy what they want from agencies and libraries established for the purpose of supplying to the press. Some have their own staff photographers who will inevitably be better acquainted with what the editor wants than you can ever be.

So it is wise to leave the obtaining of pix to the editor if you suspect the best you can provide will be less than acceptable in quality or relevance to your topic. Illustrations are not confined to photographs; accomplished cartoonists or writers who can supply their own artwork are ideally placed to offer editors something eye-catching, unique – and readily acceptable.

Chicken-and-egg

Which is more important, the picture or the story? Because the opportunities in selling illustrated articles (photo-journalism) are limitless there are many articles that begin as an image in a writer's mind rather than as a story-that-must-be-told. It matters not which comes first but there is a subtle distinction between a picture telling a story and an article with supporting pix. When the picture is the article the emphasis will be on what is illustrated; text will be underwriting, expanding, perhaps supplying historical background or whatever is appropriate. While most writers assume pix are merely useful additional features, those who occasionally reverse the commonplace and present editors with good pictures promoted by illuminating text can find a ready welcome.

Whichever your choice and however your article is prepared, the reader must know at a glance exactly what it is about. That means not only must the opening words grab the attention but the accompanying pix must also be an instant hook.

Types of picture

To have a fair chance of selling, a picture must have immediate appeal. That means even a glance will stop casual readers and focus their attention on the page. Remember that is the main purpose of pix accompanying articles and you won't forget the importance of only submitting those meeting the following criteria:

1 of high quality with sharp detail;
2 conforming to your chosen magazine's format and size;
3 frequently of happy, healthy people engaged in some task;
4 relevant to the theme of your article, perhaps with close-ups of your subject matter;
5 with an unusual slant if the market favours such pix;
6 explaining or enlightening the text;
7 a pic that simply can't be ignored!

Using other people's

Submit photographs you've taken from an old magazine as if they were yours and you invite trouble. It makes no difference if the magazine was published years ago or even if you've seen the same pix several times in a variety of periodicals. Don't copy from advertisements either. Back in 1887 the manufacturers of Pears soap infuriated art lovers by using a copy of the famous picture 'Bubbles' by Sir John Millais and adapting an old *Punch* illustration to publicise their latest brand of soap. Try such 'borrowing' and you will do more than annoy someone: the law, quite rightly, has redress for those whose copyright has been infringed.

Every published photograph belongs either to the person who took it, i.e. the photographer, or (if the magazine which bought it for use on the first occasion paid the photographer to surrender all rights in it) to the magazine publishing it. Regardless of who holds the right to reproduce the picture, if you try to sell what is not yours without permission you will be guilty of theft and attempting to defraud the rightful owner.

Modern computer technology allows clever merging and superimposing of pictures by digital manipulation so they may not be at all what they were or seem to be. Such deliberately distorted pictures are commonly seen in newspapers and acknowledged as obvious jokes – the head of a male politician transposed onto the body of a female pop star, for example.

But professional photographers and all writers submitting their own pix with copy must watch out for more sinister picture manipulation performed with the intention of defrauding copyright owners. Such picture distortion can have several deleterious effects: it deceives the reader, it infuriates editors and publishers and it sullies the reputation of the honest photographer. The National Union of Journalists now tries to adopt the policy that original 'pure' photographs should carry a 'genuine photo' mark to indicate that they have not been digitally manipulated in any respect, and magazines are beginning to adopt this system for their own protection.

In some photographic circles the buyer of the film is credited with ownership of copyright, even if the subsequent pictures were taken by a different person. This point has been known to cause difficulties for photographers able to claim expenses from magazines and newspapers, so don't be too eager to unload the cost of film on an editor who might be willing to subsidise you. Elsewhere, in certain circumstances, the person being photographed, if the target is a person, is deemed to have a share in the copyright, although (I'm glad to say) this odd ruling has never been upheld.

You see just the picture you want on a picture postcard or in an old book. How can you use it without incurring somebody's wrath? For the latter, if you can be certain the book is out of copyright you may use its pix with impunity. But still be careful. A cautious writer will contact the publisher, if he is still in business, and ask for written permission to use the picture. If that is impossible and you can't find the rightful owner of the copyright you might decide to take a chance. I don't advise it, but if you do you should at least include a credit to the original publisher when you submit the pix to a magazine. For picture postcards the same rule applies except that, again, you may not be able to find the original publisher and holder of the copyright.

The majority of magazines accept prints as well as transparencies. If in doubt about what is required, simply call the editorial office and ask for guidelines – which will often come to you as a printed sheet of helpful instructions detailing exactly what is required and how to submit it. Whatever you send in the way of original illustrations, be sure every item carries a description or caption, is carefully packed to prevent accidental damage and identifies you as the copyright holder.

Notwithstanding copyright problems, selling old pictures (as well as new) for reproduction is a thriving business for the many picture libraries up and down the country, as outlined below. You will have to pay a fee for each picture you want to use (and writers often complain the fees are higher than they should be) but at least using pix acquired through the proper channels won't cause you any headaches: it is better to be safe, even if a little poorer, than sorry.

Where and how to get them

When you submit pix to a magazine it is assumed you have the right to do so (but see below) and that the pictures are yours. But what if they are not good enough?

Here are four ways of setting to work:

1 Improve your camera technique

Modern technology boosts sagging confidence; many 35mm compact automatic cameras ask you only to point at the target in the viewfinder, press a button – and there's success. Such pictures form the majority of those accepted by magazines. Adding a zoom lens makes the target appear closer without the photographer having to move any nearer and is equally painless to use. An automatic single lens reflex camera (known as an SLR) on which you can interchange lenses is ideal. For simple operation choose one offering manual focusing. There are dozens of cameras more sophisticated and complicated but if you are a writer first and a photographer very much second the above set-up will suffice and produce perfectly good results.

This is not a book on photography so if you are happy devoting your time to it rather than writing you should seek out the many specialist magazines and books for amateur photographers, regular and careful study of which will teach you a great deal.

Beginners should stick to black and white film. To satisfy editors, almost everyone could stick to black and white. With the exception of publications specialising in colour or using it for particular displays, magazines generally prefer to deal with plain black and white. For general work colour prints are seldom wanted; the results are often substandard and magazines that do use colour pix are likely to prefer transparencies.

Whatever your camera choice, automatic or manual, always carry enough film and then some more because it is wise to take several shots of everything you photograph if you can. Although of the same topic they will differ from each other and each will therefore be original.

In photographic terms 'framing' refers to how adequately the picture fills the space available for it: we are not talking here about any contraption for hanging the picture on the wall or standing it on the mantelpiece. Filling the frame means letting your target, the subject of the picture, do just that. Always see there is as little wasted space as possible around the target. This ensures the eye is not distracted by fuzzy images at the edge of the photograph and sharpens the target itself. Here, the picture says with impact, is what it's all about – and nothing else.

What if the target is too large for the frame and a shot of it all will be unacceptably small? Simply take part of it only and let that fill the frame.

Processing your own film is a time-consuming business and can be quite costly. Writer-photographers usually find it better to forget ideas of doing it themselves and devote their time to writing and taking the shots; when it comes to developing film the cobbler should stick to his last.

Take your used film along to the local chemist or High Street developer and you'll have to wait for it to be returned, risk having it lost or even (as has happened to me twice) receive someone else's film back in place of yours. Worse, what may look like 'good' pix acquired this way are unlikely to reproduce to the high standards required for use by many consumer magazines. Gone are the hit-and-miss days when photos might not 'come out' properly, but your own work in taking the pix can easily be lost by poor developing. Remember, in deciding whether to accept or reject pictures, pay you for them or buy them from else-where, the editor's first yardstick is quality.

Far better is to approach an established photography shop where you will often find advice and help as well as a profes-sional contact print service. Ask for just a sheet of contact prints first. These are small pictures printed directly from the negatives and will give you a chance to decide which of your prints is/are best for the market you are submitting to and the article you have written or plan to write. A black and white print should be no less than 21.5 cms by 16.5 cms and preferably larger, with the surface unscratched.

2 Obtain free pix from other sources

Pictures tell stories. So large companies wishing to promote their wares are usually happy to supply writers with pictures absolutely free. There may be a hope that you include reference to the company at the foot of the picture when it is published and you should explain that you will do so although you cannot be responsible if such a reference is not printed when the picture eventually appears.

3 Rent or buy from agencies and picture libraries

Researching for pictures is as specialised a task as is research in any other field. Picture researchers have their own organisation (the Society of Picture Researchers) and most of the sources they consult are professionally organised. They belong to the British Association of Picture Libraries (BAPLA, see below). Libraries and agencies hold huge stocks of photographs to loan to customers who might include magazines, book publishers and individual writers. Some establishments offer an additional service that can be invaluable; for an agreed extra fee they will send their own photographers (or freelances whose work they know) to take particular photographs for a special assignment.

So vast is the range of photographs held by large picture libraries that smaller ones compete by holding stocks of pictures covering a certain topic – marine life, say, or mountaineering – and they often become well-known suppliers of such pix. Hiring unusual or specialised pictures can be expensive so it is best to establish with an editor before doing so whether he wants to buy the article and whether he expects you to supply the pictures to go with it.

Broadly speaking, picture libraries fall into three main categories:

A Press agencies and general picture libraries

These are wholly commercial enterprises with huge stocks to be hired by anyone and everyone. They are usually run efficiently and speedily, being much patronised by national daily newspapers who cannot afford to wait, and can obtain pictures from almost anywhere in the world. Needless to say, such services are costly.

B Connoisseur or specialised collections

These collections cover topics large and small, exotic and quaint, humdrum and precious, from far and near. The staff they employ are experts who can usually find exactly what you want. They can also tell you what you will never find, no matter where or how hard you look. (There is, for instance, no genuine picture of playwright Christopher Marlowe.)

C National archives and museums

Although Britain has a high proportion of the world's finest pictures the keepers of public institutions are not renowned for their readiness in helping press photographers. They will hire out the pictures in their charge but writers often find obtaining them is laborious, frustrating and, possibly because conservation does not sit comfortably with commercial leasing, barely worth the struggle.

Making use of picture libraries is not the sole prerogative of magazines and newspapers. Anyone can hire pix for a fee providing due acknowledgment is made for their use.

If your first contact is by telephone make sure you know exactly what you are looking for. Your request could be either specific (a picture of Charles Dickens, for example) or general but on a particular topic. You might need a selection of pix to support an article about, say, Victorian and Edwardian corsetry and will only know what you want when you see it. Call at the library yourself if you can as nobody else can make the ideal choice for you. But if personal visiting is impossible the library staff will do their best and send you the most promising selection they can find. For such work (which may take hours and involve complex research) you will be charged a search fee before even being presented with an assortment from which to choose. When you make your choice most libraries allow lower rates for multiple selection.

It is important to be clear about whether you are hiring pictures, i.e. they have to be returned, or buying them outright when of course there is nothing to return. Ask for a copy of rates and borrowing conditions before you start so you know exactly what your commitment will be. Is there a holding fee per day, per week or how does the library estimate its charges? And take care of any prints or transparencies you have only borrowed because you will be charged a high price if they are damaged when you return them. Whichever way your chosen library works, you may also be asked where the pix will be published (or you hope they will be published if you have not yet reached an agreement with an editor). Many agencies and libraries charge standard fees according to magazine advertising rates: you could hardly expect to hire a pic for *Homes and Gardens* for the same price as one going to your local church magazine. Alas, sob stories about not being able to sell the pix after all fall on deaf ears.

Always keep in mind just what the pictures you want are for. Except on rare occasions they are a support and extension of your written work, but nothing more. So be careful not to get so carried away with what you find in a picture library that the cost of the pix exceeds their value to your project. It is not sensible to let the tail wag the dog.

World picture libraries use another valuable and popular method of storing pix. CD-ROM is a computerised system which packs a vast array of pictures on a compact disk which can be read in any appropriate computer format: Macintosh or PC compatible, Amiga, Amstrad, Atari and others. In such libraries users are restricted to looking at the contents of ROM (read only memory), be that pictures, text, fonts, information or whatever the manufacturer chooses to put on the compact disk. Only when an extra fee is paid may selected pix be copied, i.e. saved, for a user's own purpose. The system has its problems; CD-ROM pictures designed for eventual printing need sharper resolution and occupy more space on the disk than those intended only for screen display. So there will be more pix on a 'black and white' disk than on a 'colour' one and the cost of 'renting' a particular picture, if your chosen library offers this service, will be lower for black and white than for colour. For on-line users the London based Hulton Deutsch Collection, called 'the world's greatest Library of photojournalism' can be found on WWW at http://www.u-net.com/hulton and you can order high quality prints from any of its 15 *million* images, with full preview facilities.

Happily, to remain competitive, picture libraries need their stocks constantly replenished and updated. That means any photographer can sell high quality pix to them as well as hire from them. If your own photographs are in this class, contacting libraries and agencies (offering transparencies rather than prints) may prove a valuable source of extra income. But be warned: the quality required for success in selling to libraries is very high. Only the best will do.

4 Leave it to others
Put photographers and editors in touch with each other and let

them make their own arrangements. When an editor asks for accompanying pictures or assumes they will be provided ('You will send me some pictures, won't you?') simply locate a photographer and put him in touch with the editor. Keep both fully in the picture (oops) and let the editor strike whatever deal he likes and pay the photographer directly for any pictures bought. That way you can concentrate on the writing of the piece and leave the pictures to other people who know more about it than you do.

Captions

Always name and number your pix. This is particularly important as your collection grows and even when you start will enable easy identification of individual prints by everybody handling them.

Keep such identification as simple as possible. The parent article can be a number, for example, with its attendant pix lettered accordingly. If your article record book lists articles by number, keeping track of what you have sent where and what has happened to it, tying your pix to articles this way is logical and keeps everything clear and tidy. Thus 14A and 14B could be pictures A and B from a sheet of contact prints taken to accompany article 14 about, for example, gravestones; 38C could be the best illustration for copy (article 38 in your records) telling the story of a young violinist prodigy. Attach small labels bearing the identification codes on the back of each pic, being careful to write the labels before sticking them on lest you damage the prints.

When you submit pix with text to an editor list on a separate piece of paper the identification codes with the captions you want to appear:

14A Lord Templetwist – high and mighty even in death.
14B Mother died first, leaving spaces for her seven children.
38C The world's smallest violin made for two-year-old
     fingers.

Keeping records

If your collection of photographs grows very large it might demand a record book of its own rather than share your article record book. There might also be pix that do not have written copy to cling to and stand as sales in their own right. It is time to open a 'picture book'. However you choose to organise it, adopt an identification system different from that used for copy so you won't confuse the two in writing to editors, claiming payment, offering rights etc. Simple record-keeping is always preferable to a complex highly technical method you can't understand at a glance when you come back from holiday and your mind's a blank.

The physical storage of photographs and negatives is more demanding than keeping written copy. But a stout file with plastic pockets will hold individual pix or contact sheets quite adequately, while smaller strips of negatives can be stored in little see-through sleeves for instant and easy identification.

Rights

Imagine photographer A takes a picture, develops it (or has someone else develop it) and sells a magazine the right to use it once in its pages. This option on a single use can be sold again and again, much as a hire car may be hired out to different people any number of times. This procedure is, of course, quite different from the selling of text where first rights are exhausted after the initial sale, leaving only second, third rights – in theory if not practice – as dwindling negotiable assets.

On the other hand a magazine buying a picture being sold for the first time from photographer B may offer him a higher fee for handing over all rights in the pic. If he accepts he relinquishes any further claim and can earn no more fees from it, however many times and wherever it may be reproduced in the future.

Who is better off, photographer A or photographer B? That depends on the innate value of the picture, how many times it is likely to sell and for how much.

When you sell an editor one of your own pix be sure to make it clear you are offering him a chance to reproduce it once and once only for an agreed fee. Never part with copyright, i.e. hand over full unfettered use, to anyone. Pictures you have taken are yours and should remain so. You never know when the subject may suddenly become fashionable, not to say famous, and then ... Imagine the chagrin if you had sold all rights in your pictures at such a time!

All for nothing?

Despite advice to the contrary (from me as well as from other people) a high proportion of articles are still submitted to magazines on spec. So are pictures, which tend to cause more trouble than copy. They get lost, their ownership is disputed, they are published without credit and too often they are either not paid for or are lumped into the overall fee. A picture may or may not be worth a thousand words but on the whole it is more difficult and expensive to replace.

In common with all writing practice negotiation with magazine editors best comes before doing the job. If there has been no editorial contact and your illustrated article is published, you might expect to receive one fee for the copy and an extra one for the pix. When this is not what you receive you have only yourself to blame; at this stage it is too late to alter the situation and you'll just have to take whatever you are given.

Since enclosing or not enclosing pix with an article may make the difference between acceptance or rejection, an editor may consider the pix form an integral part of the whole submission and therefore do not merit a separate fee. Such thoughts easily persuade him to pay, in effect, nothing for the pictures you may have taken and tended so carefully or even paid someone else to supply.

On the other hand, if you enjoy photography and feel your skills will improve with practice there might be at least two valid reasons for continuing to submit them even if they attract no extra fee: you will never actually know whether the article would have been accepted without them, and publication of your pix is valuable when you want proof of your success to show editors in higher paying markets in the future.

Some useful contacts and sources

1 BAPLA, British Association of Picture Libraries & Agencies, 13 Woodberry Crescent, London N10 1PJ. Tel: 0181 444 7913
   Publishes a comprehensive annual directory of its members, an invaluable aid for all picture users. Also a quarterly news journal and other publications.

2 Barnaby's Picture Library, 19 Rathbone Street, London W1P 1AF. Tel: 0171 636 6128/9
   Houses more than 4,000,000 pictures on a huge variety of topics, illustrating yesterday, today and tomorrow.

3 The Hutchison Library, 118b Holland Park Avenue, London W11 4UA. Tel: 0171 229 2743
   General colour library of worldwide subjects.

4 Aquarius Picture Library, PO Box 5, Hastings, East Sussex
  TN34 1HR. Tel: 01424 721196
  Specialist showbusiness library, also television, vintage pop,
  the stage, opera and ballet.

5 Photo Resources, The Orchard, Marley Lane, Kingston,
  Canterbury, Kent CT4 6JH. Tel: 01227 830075
  Specialist in ancient civilisations, archaeology, art, world reli-
  gions, myths, European birds and butterflies.

11
Business

If you have never worked in a magazine office or known anyone who has done so a brief explanation of how solicited and unsolicited manuscripts are received may be helpful. I have heard editors despair at the poor salesmanship of many writers hoping to sell their work and I've also listened to rejected writers who suspect it has been returned unread. Both editors and writers have cause to sigh at such misunderstanding. We have explored how to write each piece of work so its arrival raises rather than dampens editorial spirits. But there is more to it than that ...

The right ingredients

Just as what pleases you doesn't please everybody, so what you can sell may differ from what another writer can sell. An acquaintance sold an article about being made homeless when her house was repossessed. 'I knew that would sell,' she told me, 'because it was so real to me and I could only write it because it had my heart in it.' Practice in writing will teach you to feel as you write even if you have not personally experienced what you are writing about. In this chapter we deal with more prosaic but no less important matters: the business side of being a writer.

Throughout this book we've discussed the best recipe for success in writing. Now we talk about the only recipe for success in selling: the adoption of a confident and professional attitude.

How editors think

Try to imagine yourself as an editor. You have all the pages of a magazine to fill every week or month, or whenever frequency of publication decrees, and how well it is done rests entirely on your shoulders. There will be other people working with you, except on the very smallest periodicals, but the ultimate responsibility for triumph or disaster is yours. Filling those pages to meet editorial and advertising policy is far from easy. What happens if you are dependent on freelance copy and don't receive enough you can accept? What happens, frankly, is that you are soon called in to explain to your superiors why readers are no longer eager and circulation is falling.

So the editor is desperate to receive good copy and we are keen to write it. Isn't it absurd that we can't marry the two factors together every time? Too often the reason is even more absurd: that writers and editors do not understand each other and have not learned how to improve their relationships. I sometimes think diplomacy should be among required training for free-lances. It is defined in *The Chambers Dictionary* as 'tact in management of people concerned in any affair'. Yet many writers post off query letters or unsolicited copy, which is worse, without making the most rudimentary attempts at 'tact in management of persons concerned'. It is important to make your copy give the right impression so here are a few points aimed at pleasing the inner man as well as the outer market:

1 Ring the switchboard to ask when is the most convenient time to phone the editor or the person you are dealing with - and confirm his name.

2 Ask the editor's secretary to send you a sheet of lead times or copy dates.

3 If working after a favourable response to a query don't ring with further questions or problems unless absolutely necessary.

4 Never forget that the editor is always right.

Query letters

Listen to writers talking and you will hear opinions divided about whether to contact an editor concerning an article before you write it or to submit it in 'ready to use' form without prior communication. Although in theory and in general practice the former is the better strategy, the truth is that both approaches work at different times and for different magazines. There may be occasions when the pace eases in a normally busy editorial office and the editor is happy to read, consider and reply to letters discussing what he might like to see for future issues. At other times he could be so busy that all he wants is a complete, acceptable and 'ready-to-go' piece of work sitting on his desk. It would be misleading to lay down any hard-and-fast rule. I would not dream of sending copy 'out of the blue' but what works for me may not work for you.

As few UK magazines issue prospective contributors with a list of topics already in the pipeline for future issues, a custom favoured by an increasing number of US markets, the query letter may be a valuable aid for writers who do not want to waste time and effort preparing material that will inevitably be rejected.

There is another reason for not submitting copy 'on spec': an avalanche of unusable copy landing on editorial desks is counter-productive to all of us. It brands senders as perpetual amateurs, blocks channels of communication and ultimately makes it harder for copy with the professional touch to be located and considered.

A query letter as the first shot in your sales armoury gives its recipient an immediate impression. It tells him you can express yourself in uncluttered logic, you have a proper understanding of his magazine and its requirements and you can be relied on to supply what you offer. So before sending it you should work on it quite as carefully as you will on the copy you subsequently write. Keep the letter brief and to the point. Address the editor by name as 'Mr Smith' rather than 'John Smith' and not, at least until on familiar terms and then only with cautious discretion, as 'John'. Doubts about the marital status of a female editor are best resolved by ringing the magazine switchboard and asking how the lady prefers to be addressed.

Outline your article idea clearly and succinctly but in sufficient detail for its potential to be assessed. Include a short synopsis of how you intend to cover the subject (a précis of the contents of each section and/or paragraph should suffice) and state the intended length. Give the date by which you could submit your copy and add details of your past successes especially in relevant fields. Remember, of course, to include an SAE for the editor's reply.

Selling your idea on the phone is not easy and not to be recommended if you are completely unknown. Even when you have had prior contact with the editor or someone on his staff you have no way of judging how much attention your phoned sales-pitch will receive for you cannot know just what is happening in the office at the time you choose to ring. So I advise against trying to sell an idea this way. Too often it results in either a suggestion that you 'Put it in an envelope to us, will you?' or a (probably) well-meant promise of 'We'll think about it and let you know.' In the former case the call has gained you nothing and may have interrupted and irritated the person you were speaking to and in the second nothing further may happen.

Being commissioned

I heard a writer saying he was unsure about whether he had actually been given a commission or not. An editor was interested in his proposal and suggested he should go away, do the job and come back with the completed copy. Was this a 'commission'? If that is a precise account of the editor's response the answer is undoubtedly 'No.' A commission or contract is a firm promise of intent to publish, no more and no less, and it matters not whether it is delivered by letter, over the telephone or face to face.

Commissions are not easily won even by experienced freelances. For an editor to commit his magazine to publishing something he has not yet seen he must be convinced the writer can and will provide exactly what is wanted at the right time. Supposing the most highly-skilled writer whose work is well known and has been published many times turns in copy below the expected standard, has an accident or is suddenly unable to fulfil expectations? Ask yourself this: if you were an editor, would you feel confident in granting commissions? In today's magazine scene freelance commissions are less frequently offered than they used to be. But that does not mean you may not be asked to fill a particular spot or make a regular contribution. When that happens it is important to understand the invitation: it is unlikely to encompass a promise to print whatever you write (i.e. is not a contract) for the editor will retain the option of rejecting your copy if he considers it unsuitable. But for most such contributors the invitation does embrace the promise to pay a fee. If you are in any doubt about your position you should always ask for a simple explanation.

A couple of brief warnings: don't make heavy weather of your rights and demands: a light but privately knowledgeable approach is the best. That means you have taken the trouble to find out your legal and ethical position should difficulties arise but you keep it under your hat unless someone tries to knock it off. And remember that even an agreed offer may quickly be withdrawn if you let the magazine down.

Rights

Everything you write is born with its own set of rights, the most basic of which is 'copyright'. It reserves for you the ownership of the piece, in law, and prevents other people from reproducing it exactly as you have written it, claiming it as theirs and receiving payment for it. Note those words *exactly as you have written it* on which most arguments about infringement of copyright founder. If someone uses your idea or writes about it in a similar vein he is guilty of no infringement. There is no copyright in ideas and no restriction on writing about something already in print. If there were, the world of literature and letters would be minuscule indeed.

When you work as a freelance and sell copy to a magazine you retain the copyright in the piece but offer the magazine the first right to publish in this country, an offer known as First British Rights. You can call these 'Serial Rights' if you wish although the word 'serial' is something of an anachronism. It originally related to the publication of a story running in several parts or successive editions of a magazine, i.e. in 'series' and is less common in modern usage. There are cases where a magazine may try to buy all rights from you, and that includes your copyright, but such endeavours should be resisted. Hand over your copyright and you forfeit the chance to claim against anyone using your work in its original form as well as the opportunity of recovering any fees paid for its subsequent publication or use in any way. Be careful lest a magazine states in small print somewhere that it takes all rights – and you don't see the statement. It may also reserve the right to reprint your copy in books, other publications or anthologies. Any attempt by a magazine to take all rights without your permission is illegal so a real or metaphorical magnifying glass can safeguard your interests.

As I write this, the Freelance Industrial Council of the NUJ fears new computer commissioning systems favoured by large publishing companies could result in the introduction of a ban on all second and subsequent earnings in any work. This would mean all freelance copy would earn its author a single payment for first use – and that's all. There would be nothing from syndication or secondary or subsequent use and such an act would sound the virtual demolition of the word 'copyright.' Should you find yourself in such circumstances defined in an editorial letter you may (unless you want to assign all rights) have to respond in the following vein: that you have regularly produced work for the title for single use only (if this is the case), that you have not granted all rights in any past work and will not do so now, i.e. that you will not assign copyright in past and future work. You may also wish to assert your right to be identified as the author of your work under section 78 of the Copyright Designs and Patents Act 1988. A nationally-known *Daily Telegraph* feature writer recently received a letter from the management saying that 'in future the commissions we give you, and any unsolicited pieces you may submit and which we may accept for publication, will be on the basis that copyright in the pieces will be vested in us without further payment.'

As there are First British Rights to offer to magazines when you submit copy for its first use in any British publication (and that includes newspapers) so there are, in theory, second, third – and so on – rights to offer with each subsequent sale of the identical piece. In practice nobody will buy copy already published elsewhere, or if they do the rewards will hardly pay for the postage, so you may forget about any rights other than the first. But using already-published work elsewhere is increasingly commonplace and presents freelances with problems.

Writers determined not to be forced to sign away their copyright are taking their cases to the European Commission of Human Rights as more and more publishers are asking them to sign over all rights in their copy before being paid. The Berne Convention stipulates that copyright exists in itself in every piece of work and that no formalities are required to register or protect it in any way.

Ziff-Davis, computer magazine publishers, offer freelances contracts claiming 'all rights, worldwide, in all forms and media, whether now or hereafter known'. Writers are also obliged to 'unconditionally and irrevocably waive all moral rights [in the contribution] and shall not, directly or indirectly, perform any service for or permit the publication of any material [written by them] in any publications which are directly competitive with any Ziff-Davis publication.'

Alerted by the protests of freelances, a leading lawyer with wide experience in the world of publishing claims that 'on the face of it, a clause like the last must be unenforceable as it comprises a restraint of trade.'

Electronic rights

A whole new field of rights was sown with the enormous spread of copy submission on-line – and a veritable minefield it soon became. Material 'published' on-line is available to anyone and everyone who might wish to copy it for use elsewhere – without any acknowledgement, let alone payment, to the original author. So a major problem is how to get paid for the use of your work when it might be called up on the Internet, copied and published anywhere at any time without your consent.

Publishers do not share your anxieties. They say they cannot afford to pay thousands of tiny amounts for rights in the new media. EMAP sees the matter as a purely technical difficulty of paying writers fees for on-line repeats, particularly for short items of copy. Their solution is to buy everything outright. Taking all rights from freelance writers, they want *all* rights, moral as well, to all past and future work. Remember if publishers want all rights they surely must be worth something and don't part with them lightly.

So be careful if you get a form asking you to sign away, permanently and for no extra fee, all rights in the work you do for the title or publishing company; copyright cannot be assigned except in writing which is why your signature is legally required. If it is appropriate, also ask exactly what the company means by 'electronic rights'. Although under British law journalists have no moral rights in the copy they supply, converting that copy into digital form revives the moral rights, which is why all rights may be demanded in whatever format copy or pix are used.

It must be said that in this field the future looks troublesome. Reed Elsevier, the largest periodical publisher in the UK, is developing an 'all rights' culture to secure all profits from the electronic media for the corporate publisher, with nothing for the copyright-owning creative writer. Publishers maintain that copyright payments for use on the net would be virtually impossible to track down and collect. How, they say, can freelances expect any reward for work adrift on such oceans of modern technology?

But that very technology makes it simple to resolve – where there's a will to do so. The smallest item of copy can be simply 'tagged' with the electronic equivalent of a bar code that can be traced to invoice any on-line subscriber who has made use of it. Then it would be quite straightforward to connect the user with the copyright-owner and make an exchange of fees due. In 1995 an experiment on these lines was organised by *Time Inc* of New York and their regular freelance contributors. *Harper's Magazine* in 1996 became the first publication in the US to announce that it would make across-the-board back payments for use of freelance copy in electronic databases and several other publishers seemed likely to withdraw (or forget) their earlier demands.

Where are justice and commonsense amid all this turmoil over rights and copyright infringement? Should or must we writers acquiesce to the demands of an increasing number of magazine proprietors and publishers who want us to assign all rights to them as a simple and effective end to the problem? Only time will tell how the situation is resolved to everyone's satisfaction.

Money

Never be afraid to talk about what you will be paid for accepted copy. 'I might upset them and then they won't want me,' or 'I'll take anything at first until I get on firmer ground,' are understandable fears beginners voice: understandable but misguided. Magazine publication is a business and operates as such. Its employees, and that includes freelances, are as much engaged in a 'proper' job as are postmen, solicitors, garage mechanics or anybody else. Do you not mention the salary when you apply for a job? Are you happy to accept low pay until your employer decides you might have more? Such a weak approach in discussing money is guaranteed to keep you at the bottom of the ladder.

What a magazine pays its contributors depends on several factors, among them:

1 company policy (generally determined by the financial state of the proprietors or parent group);

2 negotiated agreements with the National Union of Journalists and/or other bodies;

3 the writer's likely future value to the magazine;

4 how little individual freelances will accept;

I'm sorry to have to include the last point but, sadly, I have found it to be valid. It is a fact that some markets (not all, by any means) offer a beginning freelance a derisory fee or invite him to state what he wants to be paid. Either way the poor writer is in a spot: if he doesn't know the standard rates he can neither assess the offer nor suggest a figure of his own. The solution lies in investigating the fees position before getting into such a predicament.

The majority of magazines have negotiated settlements with the National Union of Journalists who issue a comprehensive guide to the topic. When discussing fees with an editor you should also ask when you will be paid. Most magazines have standard procedures varying according to their publication frequency and sometimes dependent on their circulation. Payment at the end of the month following publication is common but does not always materialise. If you feel uneasy at pressing the matter with an editor ask to see or speak to someone in the accounts department. If no definite publication date has been agreed for your copy you should ask that payment be made by a specified date – in four weeks' time, perhaps, or at the end of the month of publication.

Straightening out the matter with the people whose job it is to issue cheques also gives you an opportunity to ensure yours is made out correctly. The main clearing banks issue chequebooks crossed 'A/C Payee only' to protect themselves and their customers against fraud. This is important for writers who use pen names. So if you write under a pseudonym be sure that the accounts department makes out the cheque in the same name as the person holding the bank account.

The waiting

The busy atmosphere generally prevailing in editorial offices partly explains why writers who submit unsolicited copy have to be patient. You despatch an article to a magazine and the result is – nothing.

Why does it take editors so long to choose, as their first decision, whether they want it or not? Several no-nonsense editors claim it takes but a moment to spot a real no-hoper and slip it back in the SAE for quick rejection. Others toiling under hefty daily deliveries of mail confess their office staff can't cope and it is common for submissions to stay in heaps on the floor for weeks. Some magazines find this frustrating and receive so much harassment from writers they genuinely try to relieve the situation. A few have announced they will only accept unsolicited work on stated dates and several others refuse anything that has not been under discussion. In such cases an editor or one of his staff may have expressed willingness to read the copy (nothing more, and certainly with no commitment having been made) and will provide the writer with a code number to put on the envelope carrying the relevant copy. When it arrives it can easily be sorted from other non-coded submissions and should at least be dealt with fairly promptly.

In spite of these occasional helpful attempts at easing the problem it is not uncommon for five or six months to pass before a writer is given any idea of what has happened to his work. A handful I know decided enough was enough and it was time to take a more practical line; they now put a time limit on all unsolicited work, enclosing a polite but firm note indicating it will remain on offer to the editor only until a stated date. How far ahead of submission that date is will depend on the publication frequency of the magazine but for a monthly it is usually about nine or ten weeks ahead.

You may think that is cutting off the nose to spite the face but any novel ideas you may have about how to get editors to respond could be worth a try.

At last comes a decision and your copy has been accepted. But when the news is good there may be more delay, this time for publication which may take months; I've had complaints from some writing friends who have had to wait for *years*. Advice on how to speed up this stage? Realistically there are only two courses of action and one of those is unthinkable. You can either demand your copy back and forget the whole business (well, who would do that after going to such trouble?) or you can sit tight, make polite enquiry about progress ('in case I missed seeing it') and busy yourself with other work.

And more waiting

The patience of writers is still put to the test after publication and perhaps this is the hardest and least reasonable delay to endure: waiting for payment. In fairness to magazine proprietors and to reduce to realistic proportions the number of occasions when strong action is necessary I must remind readers that most magazines pay what is due without fuss. But sometimes getting paid can be a battle which may involve threats of starting action in the courts against magazine owners or proprietors. If you reach this point (and you must be prepared to go ahead with such a plan if it becomes necessary) write by Recorded Delivery to the accounts department, addressed to the Chief Accountant if the magazine is part of a large group, telling him what you intend to do. Mark your letter 'Recorded Delivery' so the seriousness of the position is still evident if the envelope is thrown away. State that you will proceed to the County Court unless you receive payment for X script (the title of your unpaid work) by a stated date three or four weeks ahead of the date of your letter.

It is a comfort to report that most of the writers questioned in my research on this topic found the threat of court action enough to make cheques appear in their letter-boxes as if by magic.

All the same who wants to have to threaten legal action every time a magazine is slow to pay? There can hardly be any other commodity that is sold on such a curious basis; that an unstated fee will be paid for it at some unspecified time if the editor then decides he wants it; or it may be torn up, abandoned or discarded without recompense to the writer. How, you may ask, are we writers ever going to get out of this unsatisfactory state?

There are ways of improving our chances in the editorial pot. Among them are careful marketing, quality writing, painstaking research and all the other points raised in these pages. Given these elements, the single most effective additional aid is to do business in as professional a manner as possible.

Have you ever wondered why so many editors treat writers badly? I have had years of seeing both sides of this writing game; working in editorial offices and getting to know how some non-professional writers think. And I use the term 'non-professional' here in its depressing sense, meaning writers who persist in behaving like amateurs even though they are not necessarily beginners. Such folk happily accept low or even no fees for their work, having learned that some editors will take their free or virtually free copy even if someone on the staff has to smarten it up before it is ready for publication.

As long as these 'perpetual amateurs' exist there is no incentive for editors to treat writers any better than they do now – so they won't. Ah, you might argue, but why not be a 'perpetual amateur' if you can get published that way without much difficulty? Well, it depends on what you want as a writer. I could accept derisory fees or give my copy away. But I can't separate being a writer from working at a professional job which satisfies both my bank balance and my self-respect. If you aren't fussy about either ...

So let's consider some practical answers to this apparently endless waiting game editors so often make us play. Always address your cash queries to the accounts department of the magazine, rather than the editorial, thereby tackling the appropriate people while not prejudicing any future relationship with the editor. Present your invoice neatly and without frills, on your headed paper, perhaps like this:

INVOICE (give number)   (today's date)
Copy: The Stagecoach returns 1200 wds + 3 pix
Published: Buses Magazine August 1997
Fee due: £175.00
Payment date: 29 July 1997

Give the invoice a date, sign it and be sure to keep a copy in your records.

If nothing happens after a month (in the case of a monthly publication: in a fortnight if publication is more frequent) send another invoice marked SECOND INVOICE in red and enclose a copy of the first. But supposing even your best and most professional endeavours to obtain what is rightfully yours come to nought? Is it time to be unprofessional?

On various occasions I and colleagues have tried patience, polite persistence, not-so-polite persistence, downright brusque persistence, threatening to sue and actually suing. Mostly the stronger the action the better the results; it is a sad fact, and not only in the world of writing, that those who shout loudest usually receive the best attention. But several times unorthodox and 'Oh, you can't do that!' tactics have proved more effective than any of the above.

Here are a few you might care to try when owed money and sufficiently driven by frustration, starvation or general outrage:

1 If a fee has been negotiated send an invoice to the accounts department for double the agreed amount or at least more than you expect to receive.

2 Urge a recognised body such as the NUJ or the Society of Authors to publish a list of bad payers – and see the baddie who owes you money is on it.

3 Inform the magazine that you are writing a report (and do so) for a writers' journal, or similar, listing poor payers in the magazine field. You do so hope it won't be necessary to include ...

4 a) Attend the editorial or accounts office in person.
   b) Do not announce you are coming.
   c) Take with you a fretful baby, an inexhaustible toddler, an impatient dog or any combination of the three and make no effort to quieten or control any of them.
   d) Ask staff members to hold the baby, amuse the toddler or calm the dog while you sort out your papers.
   e) If you can't find live companions take sandwiches, a vacuum flask and a radio.
   f) Stay until your account is paid, however long it takes. No magazine can risk the bad publicity of having you evicted by force nor can you be left in the office alone at night with free access to equipment and telephones.

Kill fees – and worse

It rarely happens that an editor accepts your copy and then changes his mind. But it might be that he finds something on similar lines that he likes better, the circumstances in which your copy was appropriate no longer obtain or, as is his prerogative, he just doesn't want it any more. If this happens after your work has clearly been accepted either verbally or by letter you should be paid what is known as a 'kill' fee. How much this is may be determined by standard editorial practice for the magazine concerned, or its parent group, or may be left to the editor's discretion. Since it represents a loss to the magazine you may not receive much but justice demands you get something. If a kill fee is not forthcoming, and few editors will offer one unless you raise the matter first, point out the difficulties you may have in selling the piece elsewhere, especially if it was researched and angled at the request of the magazine now killing it. Be polite but firm if you want fair treatment.

When commissioned or accepted copy is unused and a kill fee has been paid for its non-use the original rights in it remain untouched. It has never been published so you are free to offer first rights again wherever you choose without any requirement, legal or ethical, to mention its history.

At the other end of the 'what should I be paid' scale (and this is advice specifically for beginners) watch out for tempting offers of publication for which *you* pay. This is an apparently easy road to seeing your work in print – as long as you subscribe to the magazine and pay for so-called free copies. Will they buy your food or settle your gas bill?

When a publisher is ready to pay good money . . . that, and only that, is a sign of the real value of your work.

Easy record-keeping

It is essential to keep records of what you send where, when and what the editorial response is. At its simplest a single lined exercise book with numbered pages will suffice.

Number everything you write and make the book's right hand pages into your manuscript records. When you despatch copy numbered 4 titled 'Fishing in Galway', for instance, take page 4 of your book, top it with 'Fishing in Galway: 800 words' and detail, in columns if you wish, where you have sent it, the date of despatch and whether pix were included. Leave the last column for completion when you hear its fate; if accepted, a plain 'A' and the fee received are good to see when browsing through the book at a later date. If the copy does not sell the first time out you use the last column for its date of rejection – and start its second journey on the line below.

The clean left-hand pages are useful for making notes that do not readily fit into any preordained column, such as reminders of people's names and preferences, often elicited from contact with the magazine during negotiations about the copy. Here I also paper-clip letters from magazines relating to the copy on the right.

As you gain experience you will find not every piece of copy needs a page to itself so you simply draw a thick line below the successful history of one item before starting another. Your record keeping may develop into a more sophisticated routine but however you decide to work and whatever system you choose, I urge you to keep it as straightforward as possible. It is never profitable to spend a disproportionate amount of time and effort keeping records, important as their safe keeping undoubtedly is.

The rewards

It is wise to keep your financial affairs in order by opening a special account solely for your earnings as a writer. This is regardless of any other accounts you may hold and will prove its value when the time comes to satisfy the tax inspector. Annual income tax returns cannot get muddled up with other income you may have and you can, if necessary, demonstrate exactly what your earnings have been. If you also draw on this 'writing' account for your legitimate expenses you will be able to total them without difficulty, making sure you set the correct amount against your earnings in any tax year.

If you are a self-employed writer (like most readers of this book) you need accurate up-to-date information on how to organise your tax affairs. You don't earn enough to pay tax? Even if this is the case now, it will pay you handsomely to think ahead to the day when your writing success puts you in the tax paying league. By being prepared at this early stage in your career and keeping careful records of everything you earn and all your running expenses, even if all this is viewed by no other eyes than yours, you will be doing yourself a good turn.

Do you know when and in what circumstances you will or may become liable to pay income tax on your literary earnings? Do you know how to relate your taxable income to any other source of income you may have, what expenses a writer may legitimately defray from tax liability, or when and how frequently you may have to pay? If the answer to any of these questions is 'no' you need help.

Lloyds Bank Tax Guide by Sara Williams and John Willman (Penguin Books Ltd, Bath Road, Harmondsworth, West Drayton,

Middlesex UB7 0DA) is written specifically for the self-employed. It is packed with help for everyone, even those folk who are not writers. Contents include: fifty ways to save tax, easy steps to filling in your tax return, tax-efficient investments and lots of guidance for the self-employed. At £8.99 it is money well spent.

McNae's Essential Law for Journalists (Butterworth & Co., 88 Kingsway, London WC2B 6AB) is called the Bible in countless editorial offices. Leonard McNae had no formal legal training but personal misfortune placed him in an ideal position to study legal problems faced by journalists in the course of everyday work. In his mid twenties he was working as a reporter for the *Sussex County Herald* when he began to lose his hearing, had to leave reporting and turned to editing. His book originated from an earlier volume written for the NUJ by lawyer G.F.L. Bridgman who had revised it after the war as a correspondence course for the training of demobilised servicemen and servicewomen wanting to become journalists. By 1953 the course needed completely rewriting and had been taken over by the recently formed National Council for the Training of Journalists. The revision was done by McNae who was then working on the sub-editors' desk of the Press Association. A year later the legal material included in the course was published by Staples Press as a separate volume titled *Essential Law for Journalists* – and a legend was born. McNae relinquished the task of editing new editions when he retired in 1967 and died in 1996 at the age of 93. Worth every penny of the tax deductible £7.99 price.

Tax

The Inland Revenue agrees that self-employed people who sell their services to a variety of customers are, in effect, without regular employment. They are therefore exempt from taxation at source and can smooth any cash-flow problems by being assessed under Schedule D which recognises that a percentage of overhead costs can be deducted from taxable income. The Budget of 1993 proposed self-assessment as a simplification of the way tax payments are organised and this, introduced in 1996/7, affected the dates on which tax is due. Its intention was to give every taxpayer a single tax statement with only one tax bill covering all annual income. Tax returns are due on January 31 following the end of your tax year or you pay a £100 fine, with a further £100 due for being six months late.

Freelances regularly published by the same magazine (with a weekly children's column, monthly gardening tips and so on) can fall into a horrible no-man's-land between being taxed at source and being allowed the advantages of the Schedule D umbrella. If part of your work is regular, argues the Inland Revenue, you cannot be considered wholly freelance. Trying to sort out the complexities of being part employed and part freelance, partly taxed at source and partly taxed under Schedule D, is a nightmare as I know from bitter personal experience. Before you accept a 'regular' job check with the magazine's accounts department that you will always be paid gross, i.e. without deduction of tax or national insurance. (The horror is compounded when insurance contributions are also deducted and tax is levied at the maximum rate, disregarding personal allowances.) If you cannot be given such assurance, perhaps because the magazine, in good faith, fears pressure from the Inland Revenue inspector and dare not commit itself to your cause, insist you will be informed if and when any changes occur in the way you are being paid. Should your Schedule D classification be withdrawn you will at least be able to decide whether the regular job in question will be worth doing if you continue.

All being well and even though you never meet nor expect to meet any problems about your freelance standing it is helpful to use headed paper carrying the word 'freelance' beneath or beside your name. Business cards should do the same. Some writers fear the word belittles their capabilities in the eyes of professional or staff journalists. Anyone who has worked on both sides of the fence knows it takes as much – if not more – hard work, determination and sheer professionalism to succeed as a freelance as it does to satisfy one's superiors in an editorial office where other people may cover for one's mistakes and shortcomings.

To strengthen your freelance status, spread your net wide. Write for as many magazines as you can in as many regions or countries as you can and in as many diverse ways as you can. This, you may enlighten the taxman should he ever query your status, is what freelancing is all about. And in case he doesn't know what the word originally meant you can broaden his education with the intelligence that the first people to be called 'freelances' were mercenary knights and men-at-arms who roamed around Europe after the Crusades working for anyone who would employ them for what were usually short-term assignments. You may not carry a sword but you are a modern-day freelance and should be taxed as one.

Claiming expenses

There are a good many expenses you may legitimately claim to reduce your tax liability. I have been amazed to find that what is allowable may vary according to where you live and what experience your tax inspector has (or has not) of other writers or self-employed people. This being so (and should it be so?) it is best to be as clear as you can be about your own position when you establish your self-employed status.

You may rightly set against tax anything you buy for establishing and running your business as a self-employed writer. This may include the following, if relevant to your particular type of writing:

Postage
Accountancy fees
Office heating, lighting and cleaning
Fees for conferences and tutorials
Business equipment (computer, word-processor, printer, fax machine, mobile phone etc)
Printer and/or typewriter ribbons/cartridges
Subscriptions to professional bodies or associations
Telephone
Photocopying costs
Stationery (including printed paper, business cards etc)
Research costs
Insurance and maintenance of office equipment
Disks and tapes
Hotel expenses
Travel expenses
Secretarial expenses
Reference books (including this one)

Amortizing the purchase price of essential equipment such as a word-processor or a camera is usually allowable by negotiation with the tax inspector: subject to the capital cost this may work out in the first and second years at 20% or 25% of the purchase price with perhaps smaller amounts allowed for subsequent years until the total sum has been defrayed.

If you do not want to make your tax inspector scoff you should be careful to keep your capital expenses in proportion to what you hope you will earn. This is particularly sensible before you are firmly established. Gaining a reputation for selling reliable work pleases more than editors: the Inland Revenue will also accept that you are a serious writer and that the claims you list to be set against tax are authentic.

It is permissible to offset so much against tax that you are actually working at a tax loss, a situation some writers are able to use to their benefit by setting a writing loss against income from other sources.

The seventeenth century French politician Jean-Baptiste Colbert had a clear view of the situation: 'The art of taxation,' he said, 'consists in so plucking the goose as to obtain the largest amount of feathers with the least amount of hissing.' But regardless of what we may sometimes believe, the Inland Revenue is not entirely without compassion. In assessing freelances with little or no income your tax inspector must be satisfied that you are working as a writer (researching, gathering material or engaged upon legitimate business, if not actually covering paper with words) with every intention of achieving publication. In such circumstances simple three-line statements will suffice and long detailed tax accounts are not required. Of course you must still keep careful records both for your own protection, should you ever wish to query Inland Revenue demands, and as evidence to support your claims against expenses should substantiation be needed.

In times past freelances taxed under Schedule D were able to claim a proportion of their domestic rates as tax deductible. Such Inland Revenue largesse does not apply to the Council Tax, it being a tax on individuals rather than on property. All the same as a writer, whether employed in another sphere or not, you may claim that the room where you write is not exclusively a 'business' work room if it is used for domestic purposes as well.

Even before you've earned anything from your writing you may legitimately claim expenses providing you have already informed the Inland Revenue that you are in business as a writer. For example, your work may take months or even years to research before a word of the finished product is written and you may carry forward a sum covering 'work in progress' for many years although this is more likely to be the working pattern of book writers than magazine journalists.

Good record-keeping pays dividends. With it you needn't fear the shadow of the Inland Revenue while also being fair to your own pocket. Be meticulous in being able to produce genuine records and receipts to substantiate your writing credentials if you are ever asked to do so.

At the start of your writing career you may be tempted to dismiss the first few sums earned as not worth telling the Inland Revenue about. Think again! No matter how little the reward they must be told. It is in your interest to tell them: there might be awkward questions to answer if you don't but when you do you are establishing a firm and honest base from which you will be able to claim expenses to set against tax in the future.

I like the story of the cheque that arrived at the Treasury accompanied by an unsigned note. It read: 'I can't sleep at night for thinking how I did not declare all my earnings five years ago and so did not pay the correct amount in income tax. Please accept the enclosed cheque for £65. If I find I still can't sleep I'll send you the rest.'

Reselling your copy

The thought of selling one piece of work to different editors causes panic in the hearts of many writers. Can this be done without incurring trouble? Don't editors mind? Is this syndication?

This is a summary of the position:

1 Selling identical copy to different editors, i.e. posting off duplicates of what you've written to various magazines offering them the first chance of publishing the piece is technically impossible. You can only give one child the first lick of a lollipop. Offer First British Rights in a particular piece to more than one editor and you will not only be courting trouble, you will also be guilty of deception. Once first rights have been sold you cannot offer them to someone else.

2 To resell your copy but still be able to offer first rights it must be different from what you have already sold. In this way you will not be selling the same piece. By rewriting your work for another market you are not deceiving or defrauding anyone. In fact you will be doing your writing experience a world of good.

To a family-orientated magazine, for instance, I sold first rights in an article about researching family history. Then I rewrote my own copy for a publication dealing with developments in computer programming, this time slanting the article to the value of computer programs in such work. This second article was, of course, quite different from the first so it earned a whole new set of rights for itself and I was able to offer first rights to another editor. In fact all I had done was write a second article out of my own first article and additional research material I had already gathered. Call this process 'rewriting' or 'recycling' or 'adapting' or whatever you wish but it is very different from the practice referred to in paragraph 1.

Syndication

Syndication is a system that does permit multiple selling of the same piece of work for readers of different magazines – even at the same time. It works on the principle that they will not be the same readers because the essence of syndication is that circulation areas do not overlap. This effectively cuts national and nationally-circulated magazines out of the syndication business and confines it to smaller, regional or local publications. In the newspaper world it can be profitable but in the magazine world it is often hardly worth bothering about. The exceptions to this generalisation lie in specialised copy written at the behest of syndication agencies some of which deal exclusively with overseas syndication. Writers whose work is sufficiently well known may find advantages in such work but it is not an easy option. Can you write copy that will without being edited appeal to readers in, say, three or four different countries? When you're aiming to syndicate to the world the what-to-write-about problem is not easily solved. (See also Chapter 7: International Marketing.)

Training

You would hardly expect to sit down at a piano and play Bach's *Toccata and Fugue in C minor* with nigh-perfection – without ever having fingered a keyboard, would you? Every musician knows the route to success is practice, practice, practice and yet more practice – and of course the same rule applies in every human achievement in any field. But because we all learn to write, i.e. put words on paper, at an early age, we self-consciously feel we should be able to write publishable fiction or non-fiction without much extra trouble. Words are our common currency, goes the apparent logic; we speak and communicate without effort, so isn't it just a matter of writing things down instead of saying them?

Writers appreciate life isn't like that and that writing must be developed, practised and understood if success, regular success is to be gained. I emphasise understood because in writing for magazines, as in every other form of journalism, simply knowing the ropes is a great asset. Although the majority of freelances working outside or even inside magazine offices have never received any formal training, to follow a course developing your writing skills (or even revealing how they might be improved) can be enormously rewarding. And when the results appear in the form of published tear-sheets and cash in the bank, you will be in no doubt about the value of training. Such learning, though not essential, is never wasted.

So where do you start? Age is immaterial whether you want to follow a course at Higher Education level, perhaps under the aegis of your local education authority or county or borough council, or whether you aim for a first or master's degree in creative writing. The Local Education Authority or the Workers' Educational Association (17 Victoria Park Square, London E2 9PB) may run courses in creative writing in your area. Sessions are generally held during the afternoons and evenings and the cost is moderate. It is wise to investigate your potential tutors' background before enrolling. While a published writer can be enormously helpful in practical terms, the ability to teach does not always accompany personal writing success. So a good writer may not be a good teacher. In most areas you are invited to attend one meeting before deciding whether to join and this gives you a chance to assess whether or not you wish to enrol for the whole course.

Postal tuition in writing is very popular but it must be said that in journalism, whether writing for newspapers or magazines, there is nothing quite like the feeling of personal involvement. This notwithstanding, there is much that can be learned from following a course, mostly in the groundwork of grammar, syntax and other basic aspects of the use of English, especially for would-be writers who feel they missed out on the elementary topics in their formal education or those to whom English is a foreign language. If you feel the need to brush up your primary writing techniques before delving more deeply into writing for magazines, a postal course could be useful to you.

The great advantage of a home study course is that in order to follow it you have to do just what it is teaching you to do – to write – and an 'official' training scheme involves plenty of practice. The National Council for the Training of Journalists (Latton Bush Centre, Southern Way, Harlow CM18 7BL) offers a distance-learning course in magazine journalism. Their preliminary examinations are a recognised pre-entry qualification into journalism and their home study courses prepare you for such examination. One of the home study courses is Writing for the Periodical Press – leading to the NCTJ preliminary examinations in journalism and law, and media law for periodical journalists.

Most magazine editors consider the NCTJ system the best but the Government-funded National Vocational Qualification programme is an alternative procedure. This is not a method of training so much as a confirmation of abilities. Basic attainment levels are assessed by the Periodicals Training Council (Imperial House, 15-17 Kingsway, London WC2 6UN) on various levels of competence. These include carrying out routine research and originating ideas for magazine feature work, planning assignments, the presentation and transmission of copy and press photography. The best tutors will be professional working journalists but freelance writers are generally welcomed as students, as are working and former magazine staffers.

For full time training the opportunities are wide and your library or local information centre should be able to provide details. The first university-based journalism training course in Britain was The Centre for Journalism Studies in Cardiff which was established in 1966 by Sir Tom Hopkinson, the former editor of *Picture Post*. Today the Centre is the largest in Europe and is well-known for its high standards of professional training. I can't deny the benefits of formal post-graduate training in journalism have brought me many advantages: the greatest was being thrown in at the deep end and having to learn quickly. For that reason I urge you to take every chance in this writing business that comes your way. What you learn through doing the job will at the end of the day prove more valuable than formal training, should you have to choose between the two. Both will stand you in good stead in the future.

Many official, semi-official and commercial courses for journalists are advertised in writers' publications. The best often require personal attendance, a disadvantage for some potential students, and the worst are little better than money-grabbers offering meaningless but high-priced credentials and a heap of old-hat advice.

Correspondence courses

Correspondence courses for writers abound: are they worth paying for? The best are accredited to the Council for the Accreditation of Correspondence Colleges which aims to maintain high standards. In the interests of readers thinking of indulging themselves I have made a close study of courses advertising their wares and have also contacted students, past and present, hearing their opinions, praise and complaints. In all cases I have been investigating only tuition offered in non-fiction and especially in relation to the writing of articles for magazines. I find a few correspondence courses are well-established, the majority provide students with tuition and help but may fall short of the mark in several respects, and a few are – frankly – abysmal.

In the first category 'well-established' usually means reliable at least in the sense of being honest and providing the service paid for. Unfortunately in some folks' minds 'well-established' also has the connotation 'out-of-date'. It must be said I found such suspicions justified when I checked 'current marketing lists' from two major correspondence course organisers. In one such list eight of the twenty-five recommended magazines had folded, seven of them more than a year earlier and a further two had moved to new addresses. Another list issued by a different 'well-established' correspondence course advised students to submit their work to (among other magazines) *Eve,* which was launched and died in 1973 and *Everywoman* which was merged into *Woman & Home* in 1966. In fairness I must report that courses run by two other companies quite unconnected with the first two take great pains to keep their marketing information as up-to-date as they can. They make the point (as anyone must and I do myself in this book) that the publishing of magazines is continually changing and students must learn to rely on their own market research to discover what is and is not being published at any given time, as well as what is and is not wanted by editors. All but two courses of this first type failed to supply details of their tutors' qualifications and experience and one told me I had 'no right' to seek such information.

Most of the courses I investigated fell in the middle range, being partly satisfactory but sometimes or in some respects of doubtful value. Their virtues include good attention to presentation, grammar, syntax and overall style and a noticeable emphasis on solving the problems of beginners. Exercises are set to cover a wide range of skills and, for the most part, are marked with care and at reasonable speed. On the debit side I found a general assumption that students enrolling at correspondence courses had received little or no instruction in these topics in their formal education; this could irritate those only seeking to improve their writing abilities.

Lastly, the 'abysmal' category and that is not too strong a word to use. One course advised students to 'turn other people's work into freshly saleable material by altering a few words.' Another promises students free books to help with the tuition, not mentioning that two were published before 1960, and recommends markets of the same vintage: none of the free books has been updated since original publication and all have been unavailable in bookshops for several years.

And what about that all important guarantee most correspondence courses in writing dangle in front of their students' eyes? It goes something like this: if you haven't earned enough to cover your fees by the time you complete the course we will refund the fees you have paid in full. So do you get your money back if you are unsuccessful? My researches found only a proportion of the students enrolling and paying for a course complete it fully: note that vital point in the guarantee about completing the course. In no case did I find any time limit imposed in which the course(s) must be completed: indeed, quite the reverse. 'Take as long as you like,' say the brochures. None of the organisers whose courses I investigated would discuss the percentage of non-finishers among their students within the past twelve months. All would have liked me to believe there were none – and no non-earners eligible to claim refunds either.

In view of such alleged success I had hoped my request for a list of students who had completed their courses and were now writing happily and selling well would have met with an eager response. It didn't. The majority of the correspondence schools failed to respond on this point at all. 'We are bound by confidentiality,' a few told me when a chance to publicise their worth and the achievements of their students might have been expected; odd, as every course brochure sent to prospective clients bulges with anonymous or 'initials only' testimonials.

Reason tells me it can be no easy task, even with the best of intentions, to train by post a cross-section of people whose background and abilities you do not know; putative students can only listen to the opinions of fellow writers and make up their own minds.

All work and no play?

When you write at home, whether in just a few snatched hours at the end of a day spent working elsewhere or as a part-time or full-time occupation, there is sure to come a day when you feel the need for contact with like-minded souls. It helps refresh your mind if you are too close to your current writing project, and it will almost certainly give you a new perspective on your work when you return to it. Writing can be a solitary and lonely business, indeed it must be, for after all the reference books have been read and all the help and advice has been absorbed it comes down to what theatre-managers call BOS, bums on seats. The actual writing is only done by sitting down and getting on with it. Even writers collaborating on a project have to do their writing by themselves. The more you write the more you are likely to succeed but you will still be alone. A break among your own kind can work wonders for your confidence, your spirits and your future prospects. Do you need inspiration or encouragement? Maybe you'd find solace as well as enjoyment in joining a writers' circle.

Writers' circles or groups, call them what you will, are numerous and vary greatly. The most comprehensive list of existing groups is *The Directory of Writers' Circles* which costs £5 post free and may be obtained from Oldacre, Horderns Park Road, Chapel-en-le-Frith, Derbyshire SK12 6SY. Some groups meet informally to pool their ideas and perhaps set competitions among themselves to keep their members writing. Others, usually larger ones, arrange for visiting speakers to proffer help and advice at meetings – and these speakers will surely be experienced writers in their fields who will be well worth hearing.

You may find membership of a circle involves offering your work for criticism by other members. This can be tricky, particularly if you feel those criticising are barely in a position to do so, and it is not always easy to make a graceful exit from such situations. For your own sake ask yourself whether you will benefit from hearing the opinions of the uninitiated. But perhaps you will find, as I have, that a viewpoint seen through someone else's eyes can be a personal eye-opener.

Many freelances claim they found their true writing beginnings in writers' circles. Sharing a common interest often misunderstood by outsiders, their members are generally extremely friendly and keen to welcome newcomers. Yes, there are a few circles that suffer from an excess of mutual self-congratulation but it is always worth finding out what exists in your area and testing the waters. Failing that, how about starting one yourself ... ? Information on how to set about such a task is also contained in the Directory.

Apart from what many writers regard as their regular weekly or monthly 'fix' of meeting fellow writers in circles or groups, there is a profusion of residential and non-residential schools and conferences where writers of all types gather to socialise and learn more of their craft. So numerous are they that I have space to mention only one – the largest, the oldest, and certainly the best-known. This is the *Writers' Summer School* held in rural Derbyshire for six days every August. There you will find what is probably the best way of all to meet other writers, learn from tutorials and discussion groups on a wide choice of topics, listen to the advice and experiences of top speakers and thoroughly recharge your batteries. Further details may be obtained from the Secretary. She is: Brenda Courtie, The New Vicarage, Parsons Street, Woodford Halse, Daventry, Northamptonshire NN11 3RE.

Frequently Asked Questions

'I can only write what I mean to say after writing masses I know isn't going to be any use. This seems an awful waste of time and effort. Any suggestions?'

George Bernard Shaw wrote a very long letter to a friend, ending with this apology: 'Sorry, but I did not have time to write a short letter.' We know what he meant. But don't be too hard on yourself. In an ideal world there would be no editing at all, for everyone, including you, would write the ideal copy straight onto the paper at the first touch of the keyboard.

Try writing something deliberately boring, like the alphabet repeated several times, and make yourself do it until what you are *really* wanting to write won't wait any longer. Or set yourself exactly two minutes of 'waffle time', watching the hands of the clock, and then immediately rush into your 'proper' work. I've known both these methods work with some folk. But the best one is to have something so urgent to say and so little time in which to say it that you can't waffle.

'I feel I will never be a good writer because I had a limited education and I don't know the right words to use.'

Don't think high-sounding words and convoluted phrases are signs of 'good' writing. The very reverse is true. Clear and concise English is always preferable and using obscure words in the expectation of attracting readers generally has quite the opposite effect: they turn away in droves, unimpressed, irritated or just plain bored. Many leading writers and hundreds of lesser-known ones missed out on normal let alone extended education. One top-rank writer told me she was glad she didn't feel happy using long words. 'I just write from the heart,' she said, 'and readers understand because their hearts feel the same as mine.'

The Oxford Guide to English Usage (Oxford University Press, Walton Street, Oxford OX2 6DP) is a handy paperback for anyone who needs simple and direct guidance about the formation and use of English words and who cannot claim any specialist training in these subjects. It is designed to answer the queries most frequently asked and is in the form of a theme-by-theme guide to correct English. There are clear and helpful entries on spelling, grammar and punctuation, with particular attention to problem words in a special A-Z section. It's a handy reference guide to all the difficulties of grammar and usage you meet in your daily writing.

> *'If I write a series for our local regional magazine about local rambling routes, can I be held responsible for people getting lost because they do not follow my guidelines?'*

Make sure your copy includes a protective sentence just in case anyone thinks of blaming you in such a case. In truth you could not legally be held responsible (and if there were any doubt the magazine would not agree to publishing your work) but a protective sentence might just warn anyone who thought otherwise.

> *'Without proper training, won't I always be classed as an amateur?'*

I'll guarantee most of the top well-known freelance writers are, in a sense, as 'amateur' as you are. So what is the difference between them and you? Just this: the state of being an amateur lies not in your qualifications but *in your working attitude*. Ignore market study, despise research and be a trial to editors everywhere and you will always be an amateur, even if you've been doing it for years: but take a *professional* view of the worthwhile task you set yourself, follow the advice in this book and others – and nobody will have any reason to be derogatory about your status as a writer.

> *'Is it all right to send hand-written work while my word-processor is out of action?'*

No – unless you are writing for the 'Letters to the Editor' section of a magazine where *legible* hand-writing is normally acceptable. (Some folk think it is even *preferable,* giving a more personal and less 'professional-writer' impression.) This exception apart, excuses about your equipment being repaired, an arm being broken or even your electricity supply being cut off render your copy unacceptable. It won't be accepted because it won't even be read! If this sounds hard – well, the truth is that magazine staff cannot spend time trying to decipher hand-written copy (which may seem clearly written to the writer but is often less so to the reader) when there is probably a pile of neatly presented easy-to-read work awaiting attention and possible acceptance. The solution? If you can't beg, borrow or hire a machine, fill in the time with market study, research, straightening out your business affairs and clearing your desk until your word-processor is returned in working order.

> *'I never send a stamped address envelope and have had some success selling to magazines. I reckon if the editor wants my copy he won't baulk at supplying an envelope and a stamp for something that will help him sell his title. Why should freelances be so humble? They ask to be trodden on!'*

In editorial offices unsolicited material arriving without a stamped self-address envelope is generally put aside, before or after consideration, until someone has a free moment to make out a label, find an envelope of the right size, stick on a stamp . . . and that doesn't happen while there are other more pressing tasks awaiting attention. Maybe, as other papers pile up on desks, it never happens at all. You may have been lucky so far but not all editorial staff are known for their unfailingly sweet tempers and your unaccompanied offering may land in front of someone too tired, irritated or downright cross to bother to respond. Why should anyone reply to something uninvited and perhaps unwanted? Enclosing SAEs is the policy of politeness – and that often brings dividends.

> *'How many words a day should I write?'*

How much ink is there in your pen or how long will your fingers type for before they drop off? In the course of straight writing, i.e. letting it flow out of your head without having to pause to consult reference books, outline structure plans or notes of any kind, what is 'reasonable' to you will probably only be determined by the hours at your disposal and your level of fatigue. One well-published writer I know averages at least 1,000 words a day in straight writing while another, equally well-established, seldom manages more than 200. Yet a third counts a day wasted if he hasn't written at least 2,000 words.

Work on a project where you have to keep stopping for the reasons above and inevitably the number of words produced in any given time falls. But don't worry if you don't write a huge amount every day. Far more valuable is the habit of writing *something* regularly, preferably daily. Remember, too, that time spent in planning, researching and all the other writing 'chores' is productive time even though you may not have a great many words on paper to show for it. Most important of all, of course, is that the words you write, even if they only total 50 or 100, are the right ones!

> *'How do I know a magazine is not going to reject my article, steal my idea and rehash it for themselves, so avoiding the need to pay me?'*

You don't. But it's very unlikely such a thing will occur. In any case what you fear is technically impossible as there is no copyright in *ideas*. The worst that could happen is that somebody else writes another article based on your idea or something like it. Editors don't bother to steal ideas but sometimes a badly written and rejected piece will stir a subconscious thought in a staff writer who may – perhaps a long time later – write a better piece on the same or a similar theme. The new article would not be a copy of yours for had yours been good enough in the first place it would have been accepted for publication.

> *'If it's possible to use the wrong word you can be sure I will do so. How can I improve my vocabulary?'*

Those of us who misuse words are most likely to fall into error when we are blithely unaware of having done so. If you don't know you're making a mistake it will go uncorrected until someone tells you about it or you realise it yourself. For years I used a word I spelt as *lasvicious*. I said it too: *lass-vicious*. Folk who listened to me and read what I wrote were too kind for my own good and nobody corrected me: they just noted my ignorance without comment. Gradually it dawned on me the word was *lascivious*, a wild, wanton, licentious word, and I'd been making a fool of myself with it all this time. Do you suspect the same thing might be happening to you? Even if you are reasonably confident of your own ability (as I was) beg your close friends to correct you when you are wrong and they'll be doing you a good turn.

More people whose native tongue is not English study it as a second language than study any other. That sounds as if we whose first language is English should excel at using it; skilled carefully-conducted surveys tell a different story. Although even professional lexicographers cannot say exactly how many English words exist there are thought to be just over a million available for common use. In addition to this a further half million or so fall into the technical or specialist category. A small proportion of the reasonably intelligent and articulate adults in this country uses about 25,000-30,000 words regularly while the majority in the same category manage with about 15,000 (that's *less than 1.5%* of the total). But the average person with no higher education or adult literary skills is probably content with a vocabulary bank balance of between three and four thousand words – a pitiful proportion of what is available to everybody in any good dictionary.

Undoubtedly the more words you know the better your powers of communication will be. With a wide knowledge of English words to choose from you can more easily express your thoughts and ideas as you wish. And communication works both ways. Not only are you, the writer, restricted by the words in your personal word-bank, readers also are imprisoned by their vocabularies – which will certainly not be the same as yours. In general our reading vocabulary is more extensive than our writing vocabulary because some of the words we read we understand but lack the confidence to use in our written work. It is up to us to expand our own store of words we hear, read and write.

For steady but sure improvement read as much as you can, listen carefully to other people and browse through dictionaries. You'll find your vocabulary improves almost without you realising it. Just to build your confidence, test yourself with these words: disaffected/unaffected, stalactite/stalagmite, billion/trillion, seasonal/seasonable, imply/infer – can you be sure of using them correctly?

> *'I am longing to take the plunge, throw away my old typewriter and move over to the new technology but I receive so many conflicting opinions from well-meaning friends I am confused. Some say I will never understand a computer, so which word-processor do you recommend?'*

First of all you should be clear about the difference between a word-processor, which will only let you write text, and a computer – which will run a word-processing program but also do many other useful tasks: keeping records in a database (think of that as an automatically cross-referencing filing cabinet) is just one of them. Most computers will also let you make line drawings and use pictures as part of their word-processing package – which word-processor-only machines will not do. Which do you want? If you are sure you only need to use words, juggle them around with ease, move whole sentences and paragraphs at the touch of a couple of keys etc *and nothing more*, you could buy a simple word-processor.

A computer, with all its enhanced features, is a bit more expensive but I can't advise you to buy anything less. In no time at all you'll wonder how you ever managed without its many extra facilities. They are not as complicated as they sound: when someone first told me a database is, as mentioned above, like a card index file or filing cabinet I was mystified: what did that actually *mean*? Not until I had one under my fingers and saw how it works on the screen in front of me, with almost magical simplicity, could I understand. So I suggest your first step is to find a friend (rather than a shop salesman) with a working machine and ask for a simple demonstration of word-processing and other helpful features. Half-an-hour with a personal demonstration can be more enlightening than a week struggling with printed manuals.

As for which machine to buy – the choice between Amiga, PC (IBM-compatible), Macintosh and other lesser-known machines is often a matter of which you grew up with or were introduced to by friends. Not wishing to start any battles I can only recommend my own choice and that of most of my colleagues (which is not necessarily the same thing). My Amiga is my first love and does all I want, including everything all the others mentioned here also do – and does most of them better – while they do not do all the Amiga does. But the majority of writers do not agree with me. PC machines are the most popular, many of them using an operating environment called 'Windows' and there is no doubt that this popular PC format (PC simply means Personal Computer) is most widely used.

By the turn of the century it is possible we shall all be wholly electronic – and that doesn't mean just using our word-processors or spell-checkers or word-counters or whatever clever devices so beguile us now.

For some of us this new golden age has already begun. Be attached to the right editorial office by the pertinent equipment, feed your copy into it in the appropriate format and the job is done. Work written on your home computer is electronically transferred to your editor's office either in the form of entire disks or as shorter individual pieces. Once you are set up with the gadgetry required to effect electronic filing the expense of using it is not great. Telephone lines carry the information at breathtaking speed (without anyone having to touch the phone) and in most cases transmission may take place during cheap off-peak hours.

One last point on the topic of computers. They break down. Not often but sometimes. Don't throw your old typewriter away.

'I'm in a muddle about when to use capital letters. What should I do?'

Studying the market is the only way to find out what the custom is in the magazine you intend to submit to. Even so there are some titles that don't seem to adhere to any particular rules or break them as often as they observe them. So the following comments apply only when you cannot, for whatever reason, discover the relevant house style on capital letters.

Doubt about whether or not to start a particular word with a capital letter may bring writing that is flowing well to an unwelcome halt. A few principles are worth remembering. Capitals, incidentally, are known in the trade as *upper case*, a term inherited by modern technology from the top half of the old compositors' type cases in which capital letters, reference marks and accents were kept. Other letters we tend to think of as 'ordinary' were, and still are, referred to as *lower case*.

Upper case letters are normally used in written English for the following:

1 At the beginning of sentences and quotations and following a point (which you may prefer to call a full stop or period): 'I am going out,' he said, 'and may not return.' (Note the second half of the statement begins in lower case because it follows a comma, not a point.)

2 Proper names, modes of address and special titles: John Smith, Trafalgar Square, Africa, Tuesday, Mrs Jones, Lord Brown, His Royal Highness, Chief Constable, Member of Parliament.

3 Titles of magazines, books, plays etc: *Good Housekeeping, Jamaica Inn, Doctor Faustus.*

4 Religious events and organisations: Christmas, Lent, Church of England.

5 Single-letter words and exclamations: I, Oh!

6 Acronyms (words formed from or based on the initial letters of titles or official bodies): JP, RAF, UN. It is worth observing that most initials in sets now thrive without the points that used to separate them. Even the full stop that was once obligatory after *Mr.* or *Mrs.* or *Rev.* has dropped out of sight.

'It is hard to find out what magazines actually pay freelances. Surely there must be a standard list somewhere?'

The National Union of Journalists (Acorn House, 314 Gray's Inn Road, London WC1X 8DP) publishes a detailed guide to fees paid by magazines in various advertising bands. These figures are only for guidance and a report from the Periodicals Training Council claims freelance fees differ widely between publishers. Because of this it is difficult to generalise but for standard editorial magazine work about 46% of publishers pay £100-£200 per thousand words; established writers may secure up to £900.

At every scale fees vary widely and most are quoted as "negotiable." Wherever you are on the ladder of freelancing for magazines always make contact with editors before filing your copy and at least ask what you may expect to be paid for work accepted. If you can discover exactly what the editor will pay, so much the better!

> Then, rising with Aurora's light,
> The Muse invoked, sit down to write;
> Blot out, correct, insert, refine,
> Enlarge, diminish, interline
>
> Jonathan Swift (1667-1745)

Index